Cambridge studies in sociology 2

THE AFFLUENT WORKER:
POLITICAL ATTITUDES AND
BEHAVIOUR

Cambridge Studies in Sociology

The affluent worker: political attitudes and behaviour

JOHN H. GOLDTHORPE
Lecturer in Sociology, University of Cambridge

DAVID LOCKWOOD
Professor of Sociology, University of Essex

FRANK BECHHOFER
Lecturer in Sociology, University of Edinburgh

JENNIFER PLATT
Lecturer in Sociology, University of Sussex

CAMBRIDGE

at the University Press, 1968

Published by the Syndics of the Cambridge University Press
Bentley House, 200 Euston Road, London, N.W. 1
American Branch: 32 East 57th Street, New York, N.Y. 10022

© Cambridge University Press 1968

Library of Congress Catalogue Card Number: 68–25085

Standard Book Numbers: 521 07204 2 cloth edition
521 09526 3 paperback edition

Printed in Great Britain
at the University Printing House, Cambridge
(Brooke Crutchley, University Printer)

Contents

Contents

Preface

The research on which this monograph is based was financed by the Department of Applied Economics of the University of Cambridge, assisted in part by a grant from the Human Sciences Committee of the Department of Scientific and Industrial Research (now the Science Research Council). We thank both these bodies for their support.

The research was directed jointly by the two senior authors as Research Associates of the Department of Applied Economics, while the two junior authors were members of the Department's research staff. The following were also, at various times, engaged on the project: as research officer, Mr Michael Rose; as research assistants, Mrs D. Dutkiewicz, Miss P. Ralph and Miss R. Baxendale; and as interviewers, Messrs. P. Batten, J. Dichmont, D. Goddard, P. Jenkins and R. Payne. We acknowledge their valuable collaboration and, in particular, that of Mr Rose during the period of the main interviewing programme. Our appreciation must also be expressed to the many members of the Department's computing and typing staff who have given assistance to the project at all stages.

In carrying out our work in the field, we received the co-operation of a large number of individuals and organisations. Our thanks are due, in particular, to the following: Messrs R. R. Hopkins, W. Butt and R. Hamilton of Vauxhall Motors Ltd; Mr R. Grant of The Skefko Ball Bearing Company Ltd; Messrs P. Lister and R. Northam of Laporte Chemicals Ltd; Mr A. J. Sjogren of the Amalgamated Engineering Union; and Mr W. J. Bird of the National Union of General and Municipal Workers. National Opinion Polls Ltd kindly made data available to us from their national surveys of voting intentions. We are, of course, most of all indebted to the five hundred or so men and women who, in total, afforded us over a thousand hours of their time in interviews—with quite remarkable tolerance and goodwill.

Finally, we must acknowledge the advice, information and other assistance that we have received from our academic colleagues both in Cambridge and elsewhere. Those who have helped are too numerous to mention individually but we hope that they will, collectively, accept our gratitude.

1. Introduction

The aims of this monograph are threefold: first, to give some account of the political attitudes and behaviour of a sample of affluent workers; second, to examine various possible explanations of the variation in voting behaviour within the sample; and third, on the basis of these findings, to offer some general observations on the changing pattern of working-class politics.

Following this introduction to the monograph, chapter 2 consists of a fairly detailed description of our respondents' voting behaviour and of the nature of their attachments to the two main political parties. We find that a large and stable majority of our workers are supporters of the Labour Party, even though there are signs that in many cases this support is of a rather 'instrumental' kind. This leads us to a discussion of the view that affluence is a factor leading to a decline in Labour loyalties among the working class, and in chapter 3 we examine this thesis in some detail in the light of the data we have collected. Finding little evidence in support of this idea, we then turn, in chapter 4, to consider two other possible sources of influence on the voting behaviour of our affluent workers: first, the extent of what we call a worker's 'white-collar affiliations', and secondly, the factor of trade union membership. We show that both these variables are associated with our workers' propensity to vote for the Labour Party, and we also attempt to assess their relative importance. Finally, in chapter 5, we examine some of the broader implications of our findings in the light of the change from a 'traditional' to a more 'privatised' style of working-class life.

The research on which this monograph is based was carried out as part of a more general study of the sociology of the affluent worker. The main objective of this study was to test empirically the widely accepted thesis of working-class *embourgeoisement*: that is, the thesis that as manual workers and their families achieve relatively high incomes and living standards, they assume a way of life which is more characteristically 'middle class' and become in fact progressively assimilated into middle-class society. This thesis of *embourgeoisement* has a direct bearing on the present monograph since it has in most versions embodied the claim that affluence brings about a change in the political orientations and party loyalties of the more prosperous sections of the working class. Indeed, the simple theory of the economic determination of politics which is implied by this thesis was regularly invoked throughout the decade of the 1950s to explain what then seemed to be the secular decline of the Labour Party as a political force. The examination of the political behaviour of a group of affluent workers is, then, in itself one way of testing the *embourgeoisement* thesis.

At the same time, it should be made clear that the more general study which we undertook was not solely, or even mainly, concerned with the political aspects of *embourgeoisement*.[1] The fact that this monograph is, as it were, a by-product of an inquiry with a much broader focus has always to be kept in mind. For considerations relevant to the main purpose of the project have, of course, largely determined the way in which the workers to be studied were selected and also the design of the interviewing schedules which were our chief research instruments.

In planning the field investigations which formed the major part of the research, our first concern was to find a *locale* for these which would be as *favourable as possible* for the validation of the *embourgeoisement* thesis. We had, from the outset, considerable doubts about the soundness of the arguments involved in this, at least in the crude form in which they were usually expressed. These doubts were set out in publications prior to the start of our research.[2] Thus, we felt it important that our test of the thesis should, if possible, be made a critical one in the following sense: that if, in the case we studied, a process of *embourgeoisement* was shown *not* to be in evidence, then it could be regarded as extremely unlikely that such a process was occurring to any significant extent in British society as a whole. This strategy of the critical case involved, therefore, an attempt in the first place to specify theoretically

---

[1] The present work is a companion piece to the already published monograph by John H. Goldthorpe, David Lockwood, Frank Bechhofer and Jennifer Platt, *The Affluent Worker: Industrial Attitudes and Behaviour* (Cambridge, 1968). It is hoped to publish a report dealing with the family and community life of our affluent workers; and a final volume which aims to give a comprehensive view of the results of our study is in preparation. A preliminary survey of the research as a whole has already been published: see John H. Goldthorpe, David Lockwood, Frank Bechhofer and Jennifer Platt, 'The Affluent Worker and the Thesis of *Embourgeoisement*: some preliminary research findings', *Sociology*, vol. 1, no. 1 (January 1967).

[2] See David Lockwood, 'The "New Working Class"', *European Journal of Sociology*, vol. 1, no. 2 (1960), and John H. Goldthorpe and David Lockwood, 'Affluence and the British Class Structure', *Sociological Review*, vol. 11, no. 2 (July 1963).

the ideal kind of *locale* for our purpose—that is, the social setting in which *embourgeoisement* would seem most probable; and then, secondly, a decision about the best 'real-life' approximation to this.

The problems which arose in this connection were numerous, but although the ways in which they were resolved are, of course, vital in relation to our project as a whole, they need not concern us here at any length.[1] It will be sufficient to say that our eventual choice fell on the town of Luton in south-west Bedfordshire, and that among the chief considerations favouring this were the following:

(i) Luton was a prosperous and growing industrial centre in an area of the country which had in recent years experienced general economic expansion.

(ii) In consequence of this, the town's labour force contained a high proportion of geographically mobile workers—workers who, it might be supposed, had come to Luton in part at least in search of higher living standards.

(iii) Also in consequence of the town's rapid growth, a high proportion of its population lived in new housing areas, including a relatively large amount of private development.

(iv) At the same time, Luton was somewhat removed from the older industrial regions of the country and was thus not dominated by their traditions of industrial relations and industrial life generally.

(v) Luton contained a number of industrial firms noted for their high wages, their advanced personnel and welfare policies and their records of industrial peace.

Once this setting for the research had been chosen, our next step was to draw up the sample of affluent workers to be studied through an interviewing programme. It was decided that the best basis for doing this would be provided by the pay-rolls of three of Luton's leading firms, which accounted between them for about 30% of the total labour force of the town and its immediate environs. We wished that, in the same way as with the *locale* for the study, the interviewing sample should be subject to certain specifications designed to favour the *embourgeoisement* thesis; and in this respect the personnel statistics which the firms were able to supply were invaluable to us. A further

[1] They will, of course, be fully discussed in our final volume. But for an early attempt at specifying the major conditions favourable to *embourgeoisement*, see David Lockwood and John H. Goldthorpe, 'The Manual Worker: Affluence, Aspiration and Assimilation', paper presented to the Annual Conference of the British Sociological Association, 1962.

advantage of basing the sample on a small number of establishments was that we could thus collect fairly detailed information on the conditions of work and work situations of all the individuals concerned. In particular, we wished to examine the effect on workers' industrial attitudes and behaviour of different types of production system, and our choice of firms was in fact made so that three major types—small batch, large batch and mass, and process production—were all represented.[1]

The three firms in question were: Vauxhall Motors Ltd, a totally owned subsidiary of General Motors Corporation, engaged in Luton in the manufacture of saloon cars, station wagons and vans; The Skefko Ball Bearing Company Ltd, a member of the international SKF Organisation, producing ball and roller bearings;[2] and Laporte Chemicals Ltd, a member of the Laporte Group of companies which at its Luton plant produces a range of ammonium, potassium, sodium and barium compounds.

Within these enterprises, we then decided to confine our attention to male employees who were working in shop-floor jobs and who were in addition: (i) between the ages of 21 and 46; (ii) married and living with their wives; (iii) *regularly* earning *at least* £17 per week gross (October 1962); and (iv) resident in Luton itself or in immediately adjacent housing areas.[3] Further, we decided that in the case of each plant we would concentrate on men performing types of work which were central to the main production systems that were in operation. In Vauxhall, thus, we defined our field of interest as covering men who were engaged in assembly-line work. In Skefko, we concentrated on machine operators involved in small and large batch production, together with machine setters and craftsmen who were concerned in

[1] This reflected our concern to incorporate into our research a full investigation of the industrial lives of the workers we studied. Current discussion of the *embourgeoisement* issue revealed a very one-sided emphasis on the worker as consumer rather than producer. However, we did not believe that in this respect we had enough information to follow through the strategy of the critical case to the point of concentrating on one particular kind of technological environment as being probably that most conducive to *embourgeoisement*. Rather, we aimed at covering a number of the most important general types of industrial technology. In this, we were guided by the classification of production systems made in Joan Woodward, *Management and Technology*, H.M.S.O. (London, 1958).

[2] Skefko have in fact two physically separate plants in Luton. These are, however, in many ways interdependent and, for our purposes, could reasonably be treated as one.

[3] This condition was relaxed slightly for Laporte workers so as to include three 'satellite' communities very close to Luton in which there was some concentration of Laporte employees.

4

one way or another with servicing machines. And in Laporte we aimed to take in all types of process worker and all craftsmen engaged on process maintenance.[1] In effect, therefore, the 'population' of our critical case was made up of workers in the above occupational categories who also met our criteria regarding age, marital status, earnings and residence. It should be recognised, then, that the decisions taken here in defining the workers to be studied are in some degree arbitrary, other than in relation to our concern with the *embourgeoisement* issue, and that this is true in particular of the numbers of men covered by the different occupational categories which were included.

In sampling our population for interviewing purposes, certain difficulties and complications arose which are explained in appendix B. However, the sample which was eventually obtained was one of 326 individuals. Of these, we were unable to contact 12 (3·7%) and 64 (19·6%) refused to participate. This left, therefore, 250 (76·7%) of the sample who agreed to be interviewed at their place of work. After these interviews had been carried out, we then asked all those we had seen if they would agree to a further interview, together with their wives, in their own homes. Of the 250, 229 (91·6% or 70·3% of the original sample) consented to this, and these men—and their wives—were then taken as being the main subjects of our research. The distribution of the 229 men among the three firms and the different types of work which we considered within each firm is shown in table 1.[2]

For reasons which are given in appendix B, our sample is not in fact a random one. Nonetheless, there are good grounds—also noted in the appendix—for regarding it as being for the most part highly representative. The one main exception to this is that the number of assemblers included is a good deal too low, judged by the size of this occupational category relative to the others which the population comprises. But this is of little consequence since, as we have already noted, the number of men in each category is itself largely arbitrary. Moreover, the data presented in the text, relating to the sample as a

[1] To be entirely consistent here we should have included two other types of worker from Vauxhall: men engaged in the manufacture (as opposed to assembly) of components and, as in the other plants, craftsmen. However, this would have been beyond the resources of the project, and we thus decided to concentrate on the assemblers as the most distinctive group.

[2] See appendix A for corresponding details of response rates.

TABLE I. *Distribution of final sample by firm and type of work*

Firm	Type of work	No. of workers interviewed	
Vauxhall	Assembly	86	
		—	86
Skefko	Machining	41	
	Machine setting	23	
	Maintenance, etc. (craftsmen)	45	
		—	109
Laporte	Process work	23	
	Process maintenance (craftsmen)	11	
		—	34
	TOTAL	229	

whole, do not show any marked variation from one occupational group to another.[1]

In addition to this main sample, we also planned, for comparative purposes, a sample of lower-level (i.e. non-managerial) white-collar employees, drawn from the same three firms. Unfortunately, administrative and other difficulties prevented the inclusion of Vauxhall, and the sample had thus to be taken from the relevant grades in Skefko and Laporte. We again limited our attention to married men between the ages of 21 and 46 but in this case no minimum level of earnings was fixed and the requirement of residence in Luton was dropped. In all, 75 white-collar workers[2] were approached and of this number 54 (72%) agreed to our request for a single interview, at home and together with their wives.

Table 2 gives some indication of the relative economic positions of our affluent manual workers and the men in the white-collar sample in terms of age, income and number of dependent children. The data show that the white-collar workers tend to hold some advantage over the manual workers in that they have higher *family* incomes (more white-collar wives worked) and fewer dependent children (white-

[1] If such variation had existed, then, of course, the 'overall' pattern of response of the sample would be a function partly of the number of respondents in each group. For an analysis of the relationships between voting behaviour and occupational group see appendix B.

[2] In Skefko, clerks, cost-clerks and 'correspondents' (clerks dealing with orders); in Laporte, clerks and commercial assistants. All eligible men in these grades were included.

TABLE 2. *Age, income and number of dependent children: manual and white-collar samples*

		Manual sample (N = 229) percentage	White-collar sample (N = 54) percentage
Age			
21–30		23	28
31–40		49	41
41 +		28	31
		100	100
Income			
(Reported average weekly earnings, *net* of tax, etc., i.e. 'take-home pay')			
Husband: Under £18		47	61
£18–£23 19s.		49	32
£24 and over		4	6
No information		1	1
		101	100
Family: Under £18		19	20
£18–£23 19s.		56	39
£24–£29 19s.		18	26
£30 and over		7	11
No information		1	4
		101	100
Dependent children			
(i.e. children under	0	17	35
15 plus children	1	28	32
over 15 still in	2	34	19
full-time education)	3	14	9
	4+	7	6
		100	101

collar couples had smaller families at all age levels); in other words, the advantages appear to result from some more or less deliberate family 'policy'. On the other hand, though, considering the amount brought in weekly by the chief breadwinner, it is the manual sample who are better off.

Considered as a study in electoral sociology, it is certain that this monograph suffers from various shortcomings through its dependence upon research in which the political attitudes and behaviour of the men we interviewed were but one very limited area of interest among many others. On almost every topic discussed in the following chapters it is not difficult to think of further information concerning their political orientations which it would have been desirable to have but which our inquiry neglected. Furthermore, our research methods were not as rigorous as might have been possible in a more restricted study. For example, a study concerned with 'attitudes' should, ideally, have used more sophisticated methods of ordering and measuring these; and again, ideally, some kind of longitudinal study would have been necessary for a systematic investigation of the process of change in political attitudes that is implied by the concept of *embourgeoisement*. Finally, there is of course the point that the workers we studied were—with the central objectives of our research in mind—a highly selected group. And it is particularly important that this should be remembered wherever material concerning our sample is used as a basis for the discussion of general theoretical issues.[1]

On the other hand, though, some compensating advantages of drawing our data from a wider study do exist. In the first place, even though our information on our respondents' political attitudes and behaviour may not be as detailed or as precise as might be wished, we do have a considerable amount of material at our disposal concerning other aspects of our workers' lives. Because the perspectives of our research were much broader than those of most studies of voting behaviour, we know something about the men in our sample not only as voters but also as industrial employees, as neighbours and friends, as individuals with certain life histories and objectives, and so on. We have, therefore, the opportunity of seeing their attitudes and behaviour as members of the electorate in the much more extensive context of work, community and class. In the present monograph we refer at several points to the findings of that part of our research that dealt with industrial attitudes and behaviour; and these findings—together with those that have so far emerged from our study of community relationships—play an indispensable role in our interpretation of the

[1] It would, however, be wrong to suppose that, in terms of their 'affluence' alone, the workers we studied represented very special groups *within* their firms' labour forces. All assemblers with two years' service at Vauxhall, and some with less, earned more than our £17 per week limit, and so did the large majority of the Skefko craftsmen and setters and of the Laporte craftsmen. With the machinists and the process workers we would estimate that we were confined to the best-paid third. In accounting for the quite small numbers of these workers in our sample, the limiting effects of our other specifications—regarding age and residence especially—must be borne in mind.

8

overall pattern of our workers' party attachments and political orientations. Again, in considering differences in voting behaviour within the sample, we have been able to take into account the social origins and occupational histories of both our respondents and their wives; and these data prove to have an important bearing on the political aspects of *embourgeoisement*.

Secondly, and perhaps more significantly, there is the fact that our wider study was based on a sample of workers which was chosen as a 'critical' rather than as a representative case. As we have already made clear, our respondents were selected not only because they met our criterion of affluence but also because the kind of community in which they lived was likely to be one where any process of working-class *embourgeoisement* would be relatively well advanced. At the beginning of this chapter we listed several features of the town of Luton which made it an especially favourable *locale* for the purposes of our research. It was a growing and prosperous centre of employment well removed from the older, more traditional industrial regions of the country. It contained a number of firms noted for their high wages and a considerable proportion of its population lived in new housing areas. Finally, the labour force of the town included a large number of immigrant workers who one may assume had moved there in search of a higher standard of living. These features of Luton are reflected in the sample of affluent workers that we selected from three of the town's major industrial firms. Thus 71% of our men were not natives of Luton or of the Luton district, and in 56% of cases their parents were living entirely outside the Luton area. Of these men who had moved to Luton after their marriage, 61% gave as their reason for moving the availability of housing, or better housing than they already had, and 46% said that they had moved there in search of better paid work. Again, 55% of our respondents lived outside of typically working-class localities, such as those in the centre of Luton or on the council estates, and 57% of them either owned or were buying their houses. Thus to a high degree our sample is made up of workers who, from the point of view of their economic aspirations, their uprootedness from family and community of origin and their residential location, might be regarded as prime candidates for *embourgeoisement*. It is mainly in these terms that the findings of the present monograph must be evaluated. For, although our findings cannot be regarded as typical of the political attitudes and behaviour of affluent workers in general, they do constitute what we would regard as crucial empirical data for testing the political implications of the *embourgeoisement* thesis.

Lastly, though, we would wish to suggest that the interest of the monograph at a purely descriptive level should not be underestimated. The workers we have studied, if not highly typical of the present, may well prove to be in many ways more typical of the future. One likely objection to this claim of 'prototypicality' may perhaps be anticipated: that is, that the workers in our sample are all employed in establishments using more or less 'conventional' methods of manufacture—whereas the industrial workers of the future must surely be thought of as working in plants with highly automated production systems. The important question here is, of course, what one means by 'the future'.[1] If one is taking the very long view, then it is no doubt reasonable to suppose the near-universality of the automatic factory. But if, on the other hand, one restricts one's range to, say, the next few decades—as we would wish to do—then the idea of fully automated industry as the dominant type appears to be somewhat premature. The best assessments would seem to indicate that during this period, even in the most highly developed countries, the more advanced conventional methods of production—and notably mass production—will, on balance, decline little in importance and that it may even be the case that the extent of their utilisation will increase more than that of automation itself.[2] Thus, we would argue, workers in jobs of the type with which we are concerned by no means represent figures of diminishing significance on the industrial scene; and the great interest which automation now excites should not be allowed to distract us from learning more about them, particularly in the condition new to them of relative prosperity.

[1] And also, perhaps, what one means by 'automation'. We use the term here in its strict sense to refer to production systems which involve an automatic and in some respects self-regulating chain of process. See L. Landon Goodman, *Man and Automation* (London, 1957), pp. 24–6.

[2] See, for example, Georges Friedmann, *Le Travail en Miettes* (2nd ed., Paris, 1964), pp. 14–22 and the statistical appendices; also Department of Scientific and Industrial Research, *Automation* (London, 1956).

2. Party choice and political orientations

The main aims of this chapter are to provide an overall view of the voting behaviour of our sample of affluent manual workers and to analyse the meaning of party allegiance from the point of view of our respondents.

The data on voting were obtained by asking our workers how they had voted in each General Election from 1945 to 1959 and how they intended to vote at the next election. We have therefore a complete voting history for each individual for the post-war period. In addition to collecting this information, we also tried to discover something about our respondents' reasons for supporting a particular political party. This was done in two main ways. First, the section of the interview dealing with politics was opened by asking the respondents whether they thought that it would make a great deal of difference which party won the next election.[1] They were then asked to comment on their reasons for taking the one view or the other. Secondly, after the respondent had said how he had voted from 1945 onwards, and how he intended to vote in the next election, the interviewer, where appropriate, asked why he was committed to a particular party.[2]

Apart from these questions relating directly to party loyalties, we also asked our respondents whether, and with whom, they discussed political matters; whether for them there were any people who were particularly influential in this respect; and whether their friends had the same political leanings as themselves. Yet a further set of questions was aimed at eliciting our workers' attitudes towards certain controversial statements concerning the distribution of power in British society. The information arising from these questions will be discussed later in the chapter. Initially, however, we shall concentrate on the facts of party allegiances and on the reasons which were given for such allegiances.

Table 3 shows the way in which the men in our manual and white-collar samples voted in the General Elections of 1955 and 1959 and the

[1] It will be remembered that the interviews mostly took place in 1963–4 when a General Election was constitutionally imminent.
[2] In those cases where there was no clear attachment to any one party, the respondent was asked about the reasons for his past changes or future uncertainty.

TABLE 3. *Voting in General Elections 1955, 1959, and voting intention 1963–4: manual and white-collar samples*

	Lab.	Cons.	Lib.	Abst.	D.K.	Totals	N
			Percentage				
Manual							
General Election 1955	75	13	2	10	0	100	175[a]
General Election 1959	71	15	3	11	0	100	211[b]

	Lab.	Cons.	Lib.	Uncertain (incline to Lib. or Abst.)	Abst.	D.K.	Totals	N
				Percentage				
Voting intention 1963–4	71	12	6	1	3	7	100	223[c]

	Lab.	Cons.	Lib.	Abst.	D.K.	Totals	N
			Percentage				
White collar							
General Election 1955	32	54	12	2	0	100	41[d]
General Election 1959	28	52	14	6	0	100	50[e]

	Lab.	Cons.	Lib.	Uncertain (incline to Lib. or Abst.)	Abst.	D.K.	Totals	N
				Percentage				
Voting intention 1963–4	31	56	10	0	2	2	101	52[f]

[a] One respondent declined to answer and 53 respondents were either ineligible or unable to vote.
[b] One respondent declined to answer and 17 respondents were either ineligible or unable to vote.
[c] One respondent declined to answer and one respondent was still ineligible to vote. No information was available for four respondents.
[d] Thirteen respondents were ineligible to vote.
[e] Four respondents were ineligible to vote.
[f] No information was available for two respondents.

NOTE. The base numbers for percentaging all subsequent tables relating to these data are those given in the last column above. Also, unless otherwise indicated, the data presented in this and the following chapters refer to our sample of affluent manual workers.

TABLE 4. *Voting for three main parties in General Elections 1955, 1959 and voting intention 1963–4: manual and white-collar samples*

	Lab.	Cons.	Lib.	Totals	N
	Percentage				
Manual					
General Election 1955	83	15	2	100	157
General Election 1959	80	16	4	100	188
Voting intention 1963–4	79	14	7	100	199
White collar					
General Election 1955	32	55	13	100	40
General Election 1959	30	55	15	100	47
Voting intention 1963–4	32	58	10	100	50

way in which, when interviewed in 1963–4, they intended to vote in the next election. Table 4 gives a picture of how support was shared between the three main parties at the same dates.[1]

It is at once apparent that, despire their affluence, the manual workers we studied are as a group decidedly left-wing in their political loyalties. Over 70% of them voted for Labour in both 1955 and 1959 and a similar proportion intended to vote Labour again at the time of the interviews. Considering the distribution of votes among the three main parties, not less than 79% of our affluent workers supported Labour on each occasion.

By contrast, our white-collar workers are, as might be expected, predominantly committed to the Conservative and Liberal Parties. However, it should be noted that the Labour vote of the nonmanual sample is markedly greater than the Conservative vote of the manual sample; and that, in this sense, the nonmanual workers form a much less coherent political entity than do the manual workers.[2]

[1] Those who said they were unable to vote have been excluded from the totals. In all subsequent tables this category, where relevant, is referred to simply as 'unable' and the overwhelming majority is made up of those who were in fact ineligible to vote, mainly on grounds of age. For example, in the General Election of 1955, 53 men were classed as unable to vote. Of these, 49 were ineligible. We have no reason to believe that the men who were eligible to vote but who said that they could not do so, were not in fact genuinely unable to vote. To include them in with the abstainers would in any case make no significant difference to the findings which are presented in the following chapters.

[2] Although we are not concerned with explaining such differences at this stage, it may be said that this particular sample of nonmanual employees on the lowest rungs of the white-collar ladder is, as one might expect, more heavily recruited from manual origins than the manual sample is recruited from nonmanual origins. As we shall argue later, the fact of social origin is a very important element in the determination of party choice;

TABLE 5. *Voting intentions of men aged 21–46 in manual occupations*

	Voting intention			
	Lab.	Cons.	Lib.	Total
	Percentage			
Luton sample, 1963–4	79	14	7	100
NOP national survey, 1963	67	26	7	100

The relatively high Labour vote of our affluent workers is likely to be due to some extent to the fact that the sample was limited to men, and to those aged between 21 and 46. But even allowing for the tendency of women and of older persons[1] to be rather more Conservative—a tendency which should not be exaggerated—the average 80% Labour vote of our sample in 1955, 1959, and 1963 is still remarkably high in comparison with the level of Labour voting in the working class as a whole. A careful study by Alford reveals that, on the basis of several surveys made in Great Britain during the period 1950–62, the proportion of Labour supporters among the working class was never higher than 67% and never lower than 57%, while the corresponding figures for Conservative supporters were 35% and 24%. In national surveys carried out during 1955 and 1959, the Labour vote was between 60% and 65% and the Conservative between 30% and 32%.[2] These figures correspond closely to those generally regarded as typical of the working class in the post-war period as a whole.[3]

and the greater heterogeneity in the social background of the nonmanual sample goes a long way to explain its less distinctive political stance.

[1] On the relationship between age and voting, see Robert A. Alford, *Party and Society* (Chicago, 1963), pp. 159–68; also Philip Abrams and Alan Little, 'The Young Voter and British Politics', *British Journal of Sociology*, vol. 16, no. 2 (June 1965). It has been suggested that the tendency of older persons to be more Conservative is likely to be a 'generational' rather than an 'ageing' effect. This is certainly consistent with our findings, which show that the proportion of men voting for the Labour Party increases from 67% in the youngest age group (21–30) to 75% in the oldest age group (41–46), the figure for the intermediate age group (31–40) being 70%. See also appendix D, table D1. On differences between the voting behaviour of men and women, see, for example, W. G. Runciman, *Relative Deprivation and Social Justice* (London, 1966), p. 173, and Richard Rose, *Politics in England* (London, 1965), pp. 61–2.

[2] The figures quoted refer to the Labour vote as a proportion of votes cast or intended for the three main parties, and are thus directly comparable with those given in table 4. See Alford, *Party and Society*, pp. 348–9.

[3] See, for example, J. Blondel, *Parties and Leaders* (London, 1963), chapter 3, and D. E. Butler and Richard Rose, *The British General Election of 1959* (London, 1960), p. 10.

TABLE 6. *Classification of manual and white-collar samples by 'voting history' 1945–59*

Voting history[a]	Manual[b] (N = 211)	White collar[c] (N = 52)
	Percentage	
'Solid' Labour	62	23
'Solid' Conservative	9	36
'Solid' Liberal	0	6
'Irregular' Labour	6	2
'Irregular' Conservative	3	4
'Irregular' Liberal	1	0
Other	20	29
TOTALS	101	100

[a] 'Solid' = voted whenever eligible and always for the same party. 'Irregular' = always voted for the same party, but may have abstained as often as voted (but not more often).

[b] One respondent declined to answer, and 17 respondents were unclassifiable because they were not eligible to vote until after 1959.

[c] Two respondents were unclassifiable because they were ineligible to vote until after 1959.

A full account of the basis of this classification is given in appendix C.

More direct proof of the exceptionally strong support for Labour among our sample is provided by table 5. Here the voting intentions of our affluent workers are compared with those of a sample of men aged between 21 and 45, and employed in well-paid manual work, who were interviewed in the course of national surveys in 1963.[1] From this table it can be seen that the proportion of intending Labour voters among our affluent workers is still relatively high even when our sample is compared with a national one that is matched for age and sex, and, in some degree, for socio-economic position.

The Labour majority in our sample is also strong in the sense that a high proportion of the Labour voters are stable supporters of the party. This may be seen from table 6, where the manual and white-collar samples are classified according to the voting histories of each individual during the period 1945–59. Thus 68% of our affluent workers have never voted for any other party than the Labour Party, and 62%

[1] These figures, which were kindly made available to us by the National Opinion Poll, are based on three consecutive surveys of the electorate during the period October to December 1963. The men in the sample were skilled manual workers, earning between £14 and £22 per week, and in the age group 21–45. In our own sample there were in fact only 6 men over the age of 45.

15

TABLE 7. *Voting in General Election 1959 by voting in General Election of 1955*

		Voting in General Election 1959						
		Lab.	Cons.	Lib.	Abstain	Unable	Totals	N[a]
		Percentage						
Voting in General Election 1955	Lab.	95	1	2	1	1	100	131
	Cons.	9	83	0	9	0	101	23
	Lib.	0	33	67	0	0	100	3
	Abstain	28	22	11	39	0	100	18
	Unable	34	11	0	25	30	100	53

[a] N = 228. See note [b], table 3.

have voted for Labour on every occasion on which they were eligible to vote.

Further evidence of the stable nature of the manual workers' support for Labour is presented in tables 7 and 8. Table 7 cross-classifies voting in the General Elections of 1955 and 1959; and table 8 makes a similar comparison between voting in the General Election of 1959 and voting intentions in 1963–4. In both cases, the figures show, in percentage terms, how the votes cast for a particular party at the earlier dates were distributed at the later dates. Thus it can be seen that of those men who voted Labour in 1955, 95% voted Labour again in 1959; and that of those who voted Labour in 1959, 91% intended to vote the same way in 1963–4. By contrast, the Conservative voters in the sample were less stable. Of those who voted Conservative in 1955, 83% did so again in 1959, but only 63% of the Conservative voters of 1959 intended to vote for the party again in 1963–4.

Having established that our workers have a relatively high and stable Labour vote, we now come to consider the reasons they gave for their party attachments. During the course of the interview, the respondent whose voting history and voting intention indicated that he was a regular voter for a particular party was asked: 'Now you seem pretty attached to the Conservative/Labour/Liberal Party. Can you tell me why this is?' Table 9 sets out the reasons which were given in reply to this question by those men who were attached to the Labour Party, and table 10 shows the responses of the regular Conservative supporters. In those cases where, largely because of frequent abstention, the

16

TABLE 8. *Voting intention by voting in General Election 1959*

		Lab.	Cons.	Lib.	Uncertain (incline to Lib. or abstain)	Abst.	D.K.	Totals	N[a]
					Voting intention				
					Percentage				
Voting in General Election 1959	Lab.	91	2	3	0	1	3	100	148
	Cons.	13	63	7	3	7	7	100	30
	Lib.	33	0		50	0	17	100	6
	Abstain	43	9	17	0	13	17	99	23
	Unable	50	19	0	6	0	25	100	16

[a] N = 223. See note [c], table 3.

respondent could not be regarded as being 'attached' to any particular party, he was asked to give reasons for his lack of commitment. Men who had actually changed from voting Labour to voting Conservative, and vice versa, were asked to explain why this had happened.[1]

Table 9 shows that, among the reasons given by Labour supporters, the perception of the Labour Party as the party of the 'working man' or of the 'working class' predominated. Almost 60% of these men gave this as one, or as the sole, reason for their attachment to the Labour Party. The following comments, taken from the interview schedules, are typical of the responses of those giving this type of reason:

'I should say that the Labour Party is more for the working class than the upper class. I think, if I vote Conservative, what've I got to conserve? I just rely on the clock for a living, and if they shut the gates on me, I'm out.'

'As I belong to the working class, I feel it's my duty to support any organisation that I feel will further the aims of the working class. The average voter votes more intelligently than twenty years ago. Still, if any party really seemed to serve the interests of the working class better, I wouldn't hesitate to vote for them.'

'They [the Labour Party] are always inclined to do that bit more for the working man. My opinion of Tory government is that they're for the capitalists. If we are to achieve anything for working people, the Labour Government will get that for us.'

[1] The men who were classified as 'attached' to a particular party were in the main those whom we have referred to above as 'solid' or 'irregular' voters. Thus of the 145 men who were classed as having an attachment to Labour, 143 were either 'solid' (131) or 'irregular' (12) Labour voters in terms of their voting history. And of the 23 men classed as having an attachment to the Conservative Party, 22 were either 'solid' (16) or 'irregular' (6) voters. See appendix C.

TABLE 9. *Reasons for attachment to Labour Party: manual and white-collar samples*

Class of reason	Manual (N = 145)	White collar (N = 13)
	Times mentioned	
General 'working-class' identification with Labour (or against Conservative)	86	4
Favours social and welfare services included in Labour Party programme	19	5
Family tradition	18	3
Better off economically under Labour (or worse off under Conservatives)	16	3
Favours more economic planning and nationalisation	10	2
Labour have men to do the job; approves of Labour men	5	1
Would like to see change; would like to see Labour given a chance	4	2
Really wants to vote Liberal, but no candidate	3	1
Other miscellaneous pro-Labour or anti-Conservative reasons	32	5
ALL REASONS	193	26
No clear reason given, D.K.	13	1

'I don't go to no party meetings, but I still think they are the government for the working class; the Conservatives are just there for their class. I think going back it was the working class that first brought the Labour Party in. They'd have us at heart more than the Conservatives will.'

'I consider myself a working man, so a working man should always vote Labour. They say Labour is for the working man, to try and better the working man, and that's more or less the reason. We've had it rough under a Tory government in years gone by and it's been drummed into us as kids, the hard times. I'd be the first to vote Tory, though, if a Labour government started mucking us about.'

A diffuse class loyalty to Labour, coupled with anti-Conservative sentiments figured largely, then, in the replies given by Labour supporters. At the same time, though, it should be noted that some of these replies were couched in such a way as to indicate that the respondent did not feel that there was a great deal to choose between the two main parties, but that on balance the Labour Party was just that bit more for the 'working man'.[1] 'They have the worker more at heart' was a frequent comment.

However, the saliency of the view that the Labour Party is essentially a class party suggests that the grounds for the high left-wing voting in our sample of affluent workers are not markedly different from those of the working class generally.[2] It may also be noted from table 9 that in addition to support for Labour being regarded by a great many of our workers as a natural consequence of their being 'working class', a second category of reasons having to do with a 'family tradition' of voting Labour was of a similar, class-based and affective kind. Among our affluent workers, these two categories of reasons for supporting Labour accounted for 50% of all reasons given. By contrast, among the white-collar workers who were attached to the Labour Party, such reasons accounted for only 26% of all reasons given.

The next most important group of reasons given by our respondents for favouring Labour carried a somewhat different emphasis. These had to do with the expected beneficial consequences of a Labour government, whether for the respondent personally, or for 'working men' as a whole, or for the country in general. About a quarter of all reasons offered referred to such beliefs as the following: that under the Labour Government things would improve economically; that Labour stood for improved social and welfare services; that Labour would introduce needed economic planning and control; and that Labour had the best team of leaders to run the country. Among the white-collar sample, such reasons were clearly the more common, and accounted for some 40% of all reasons for favouring a Labour government.

Finally, a number of our affluent workers gave reasons for supporting Labour that had to be classified as 'other pro-Labour (or anti-Conservative)'. These were highly heterogeneous. A number of them related to specific personal experience, as in the two following examples:

'When my sister was in college the means test was on—as soon as she started to teach they [i.e. the Conservatives] knocked my father's income down and my father was out of work at the time.'

[1] 29% of those men who were 'attached' to Labour said that it would not make much difference which party won the next General Election (as opposed to 35% of those men who were 'attached' to the Conservatives).

[2] Abrams, for example, has reported, on the basis of a national survey carried out in 1960, that Labour is regarded by the large majority of its adherents as being essentially a 'class' party. See Mark Abrams and Richard Rose, *Must Labour Lose?* (London, 1960), pp. 12–14.

The affluent worker: political attitudes

'When they had a Conservative council [i.e. in Luton] they put the price of houses up according to your wages. Now if you've got a decent job it's on your own initiative. Why should you suffer for someone that doesn't bother?'

Other reasons included under this heading involved more general considerations; for example, that the Labour Party was the only party with a conscience, that it would have a freer hand in promoting Private Members' Bills, that it would bring about racial integration and true socialism, that it would stop the outflow of scientists to other countries, and so on. More negatively, it was held that the Conservatives wanted to abolish trade unions, that Conservative Government led to war, and that the Conservatives spent too much on the Royal Family. The total of 'other pro-Labour (and anti-Conservative) reasons' accounted for less than one-fifth of all reasons given. Moreover, since they were most frequently introduced as addenda to reasons falling into one or other of the categories previously mentioned, their main interest is perhaps in indicating the variety of political beliefs that is to be found among a small sample of the electorate.

Turning now to reasons for supporting the Conservative Party, it may be seen from table 10 that among our affluent workers the most important class of reasons related to the beliefs that under a Conservative Government things were better economically and that the Conservatives had the best team of men to run the country. Answers on these lines accounted for almost half of all reasons given for supporting the Conservatives. Another 16% of these reasons referred to diffuse approval of the Conservatives and/or antipathy to Labour. By contrast, the more 'deferential' orientation that is known to be held by some working-class Conservatives was not very evident in our sample.[1] Only 4 men out of 23 'stable' Conservative voters gave reasons— mostly relating to the superior quality of their party's leadership— which were of a clearly 'deferential' nature. The following quotations are typical of the general run of answers, which tended to express a more pragmatic and instrumental attachment:

'I couldn't care less about politics, except for one or two little things. I base all this [i.e. supporting the Conservative Party] on the fact that I've got a house while the Conservatives were in power, and found many things easier, money and hire purchase and that sort of thing.'

[1] See R. T. McKenzie and A. Silver, 'Conservatism, Industrialism, and the Working Class Tory in England', *Transactions of the Fifth World Congress of Sociology* (Louvain, 1964), vol. III, pp. 191–202.

TABLE 10. *Reasons for attachment to Conservative Party: manual and white-collar samples*

Class of reason	Manual (N = 23)	White collar (N = 23)
	Times mentioned	
Better off economically under Conservatives (or worse off under Labour)	6	4
Conservatives have men to do the job; approves of Conservative men	6	4
General approval of Conservative Party (or dislike of Labour)	4	6
Family tradition	2	4
Against economic planning and nationalisation	1	11
No experience of Labour in power; stick to Conservatives	1	0
Supports Conservative emphasis on individual responsibility	0	1
Really wants to vote Liberal, but no candidate	0	2
Other miscellaneous pro-Conservative or anti-Labour reasons	5	8
ALL REASONS	25	40
No clear reason given, D.K.	4	0

'Why do I support the Conservatives? Because I think they're the best party to run the country. Their present run of office has been quite satisfactory to me. I think they're running on the right line. I believe they're giving a fair share to all.'

'Well, I think they [i.e. the Conservatives] have done as much for the country as anybody—I mean I think their policy "you've never had it so good" is right really when you look at it. Whether it's us living in a boom town, I don't know...'

'I think the reason why I support the Conservatives is because I haven't had a great deal of experience of the Labour Party. I was only a child when they was in power, and they haven't showed me anything. The Conservative Party has been in power the best part of my life, when I really started to take an interest. I'm not actually what you would call a Conservative, but I've done well under the Conservatives, so while you're doing well I think it's silly to change. Our standard of living has been improving since we've been married. If it'd been the other way round I'd vote Labour. That shows how much I am for one party.'

By contrast with these working-class Conservatives, the white-collar workers who were attached to the party gave relatively fewer reasons expressing their approval of the Conservatives and more reasons having to do with their dislike of the policies of the Labour Party— particularly, its emphasis on economic planning and controls, and nationalisation. Over a quarter of all reasons given by the white-collar group were of this type. Again, another quarter of reasons, as might be expected, related to a general, largely 'class-based', identification with the Conservative Party and to family background.

Thus while the Conservative supporters among our affluent workers were more inclined to emphasise the Party's ability to bring about favourable economic conditions, the white-collar Conservatives seemed to be more influenced by anti-Labour sentiments, and by considerations of class and social origin.[1]

In addition to asking our respondents why they were attached to a particular party, we attempted to find out something about their attitudes towards party politics in general. The section of the interview dealing with politics was opened by the question: 'It seems likely that there will be a General Election soon—Do you think it will make a great deal of difference whether the Conservatives or Labour win, or won't it make much difference which side wins?' This question was then followed by a further question which asked either 'In what ways would it make a difference?' or 'Why do you feel that it won't make much difference?' In reply to the first question, 34% of our affluent workers (compared with 30% of the white-collar sample) said that it would not make much difference which party won the election. Approximately the same proportion of intending Labour and Conservative voters took this view (28% and 30% respectively). The reasons given for this attitude by the manual workers—grouped by their voting intention—are set out in table 11. In the main they justified their position by arguing that both parties were the same or that politics made very little difference to the man in the street. On this point again, Labour and Conservative supporters did not differ substantially and the same two reasons were also the ones most frequently expressed by those intending to vote Liberal or to abstain.

[1] Finally, the men whose voting histories indicated no clear attachment to either of the main parties (mainly owing to high rates of abstention) attributed their behaviour chiefly to apathy, laziness, forgetfulness or inconvenience.

TABLE II. *Reasons given for believing that it will not make much difference which party wins the next General Election by voting intention*

	Voting intention	
Class of reason	Labour (N = 45)	Conservative (N = 8)
	Times mentioned	
Both parties are the same	20	4
Politics make no difference to the individual (or to the 'working man')	19	2
General scepticism about politicians	9	0
Nothing that politicians can do	5	2
Other reasons	2	1
ALL REASONS	55	9
No clear reason given, D.K.	0	1

In asking those men who said that it would make a difference which party won why they thought this was so, we were, of course, directing their attention to more proximate and current issues than when we asked them to account for their party attachments in the light of their voting histories. This is reflected in table 12, where it can be seen that the general 'working-class' orientation so prominent above now accounts for only 9% of all reasons given by those men who were intending to vote Labour. Of far greater importance for Labour adherents were reasons associated with the belief that a Labour Government would improve economic conditions and welfare services. Reasons of this kind, relating to the 'pay-off' from a Labour victory, rather than reasons expressive of working-class solidarity, accounted for 53% of all reasons given; and if to these we add reasons connected with a belief in greater planning and more nationalisation as methods of economic improvement, the total then amounts to 62% of all reasons.[1] The Conservative voters among our affluent workers were less inclined to mention the expected economic benefits of continuing Conservative Government than to refer to the likely adverse consequences of Labour's emphasis on planning and nationalisation. Here in contrast to the reasons they gave for their long-term attachment to the Conservative

[1] Intending Labour voters who thought that if there was a Labour Government the country would be economically worse off had in mind the difficulties facing a Labour Government, not its incompetence. For example, 'I think the country would fall back a bit—I should think these Conservatives, big politicians with money'd take their money out of the country and put Labour in a big spot'.

TABLE 12. *Reasons given for believing that it will make a difference which party wins the next General Election by voting intention*

	Voting intention	
Class of reason	Labour (N = 113)	Conservative (N = 19)
	Times mentioned	
Better off economically under Conservatives (or worse under Labour)	2	7
Better off economically under Labour (or worse under Conservatives)	47	0
Anti-planning, control, centralisation (including anti-nationalisation)	5	12
Pro-planning, control, centralisation (including pro-nationalisation)	15	0
Anti-social and welfare services	0	1
Pro-social and welfare services	44	1
Labour more for working man (or Conservatives more for business)	15	0
Other pro-Labour (or anti-Conservative)	39	1
Other pro-Conservative (or anti-Labour)	4	9
ALL REASONS	171	31
No clear reason given, D.K.	13	2

Party, the working-class Tories were clearly much closer in their attitudes to the white-collar Conservatives; that is, in the common aversion which is shown to 'Socialist planning', and to nationalisation in particular.

So far, then, we have seen that our respondents' explanations of their party commitments present a more or less conventional picture. The Labour supporters, in particular, do not appear to be markedly different in their political outlook from the general run of working-class Labour voters. They feel that the Labour Party is the party of the working man and as working men they expect that a Labour Government would improve their economic position and that of the country as a whole, and that it would also provide better social services. At the same time, one-third of the Labour supporters were not so firmly identified with their party as to believe that it would make a great deal of difference whether a Labour or a Conservative Government ruled the country.

We may now examine political orientations from a slightly different viewpoint by turning to the answers which were given to four questions in our interview schedule that dealt with what we might call 'perceptions of power'. In the course of the interview our respondents were asked the following series of questions.

'Some people say that there's one law for the rich and another for the poor—would you agree or disagree on the whole?'

'As you know, most trade unions support the Labour Party; do you approve of this, or do you think that they ought to keep themselves separate?'

'Some people say that the trade unions have too much power in the country; would you agree or disagree, on the whole?'

'Some people say that big businessmen have too much power in the country; would you agree or disagree, on the whole?'

In a previous study[1] we found that, out of a range of questions dealing with broad social and political issues, these four were the ones on which skilled manual workers were most sharply divided in their attitudes from white-collar employees and small businessmen. It may also be assumed that more traditional industrial workers would emphatically disagree that 'trade unions have too much power in the country', just as they would overwhelmingly agree that 'there is one law for the rich and another for the poor', that 'trade unions should support the Labour Party',[2] and that 'big businessmen have too much power'. In other words, this set of questions provides us with a measure of the intensity of working-class consciousness and thus gives another perspective on the nature of the sentiments underlying our affluent workers' party loyalties.

Table 13 gives the proportions of manual and nonmanual workers who agreed or disagreed with the four statements. We may note first of all that on the question of the power of big-business men an equally high proportion of both our affluent manual and white-collar workers agree that big businessmen do have too much power in the country. Secondly, a majority of both the blue- and white-collar workers agreed that there is one law for the rich and another for the poor. Furthermore, and more surprisingly, the manual workers (by a small majority) also agreed with the white-collar workers that the trade unions and the Labour Party should be kept separate. It was, in fact, only on the question touching directly on trade union power that majority opinion in the two groups was actually opposed. But here too

[1] An unpublished pilot survey carried out in the city of Cambridge in 1962.
[2] In the Liverpool study of dockworkers, for example, only 17% of those interviewed said that they disapproved of the close association between the trade unions and the Labour Party. See University of Liverpool, Department of Social Science, *The Dock Worker* (Liverpool, 1954), p. 132.

TABLE 13. *Political attitudes: manual and white-collar samples*

Questions		Manual (N = 229)	White collar (N = 54)
		Percentage	
One law for rich and	Agree	72	59
another for poor	Disagree	26	39
	D.K.	1	2
		99	100
Trade union support	Approve	42	26
for Labour Party	Keep separate	55	74
	D.K.	3	0
		100	100
Trade union power	Too much	43	72
	Disagree	54	24
	D.K.	3	4
		100	100
Big-business power	Too much	60	63
	Disagree	36	37
	D.K.	4	0
		100	100

it was only by a bare majority that the manual workers rejected the view that trade unions have too much power. Taken as a whole, then, the responses of our affluent workers to these four questions do not indicate an ideology of power that is totally different from that of the white-collar sample. We may note in particular the relatively weak 'working-class' orientation of our manual respondents in respect of their attitudes to the power of trade unions and to the relationship between trade unions and the Labour Party. Their replies to these two questions are hardly the ones that might be expected of more traditional 'class-conscious' workers, for whom the Labour Party and the trade unions are simply different arms of a united Labour movement.

Table 14 shows the responses to the same four questions, this time controlled for voting intention. We find that Labour and Conservative supporters among our affluent workers disagree systematically on every question. It may be noted, however, that no more than 52% of intending Labour voters express approval of the existing relationship between the trade unions and the Labour Party. This implies that a

TABLE 14. *Political attitudes by voting intention*

Political attitudes		Labour (N = 158)	Conservative (N = 27)
		Voting intention	
		Percentage	
One law for rich and	Agree	78	44
another for poor	Disagree	21	56
	D.K.	1	0
		100	100
Trade union support	Approve	52	15
for Labour Party	Keep separate	44	85
	D.K.	3	0
		99	100
Trade union power	Too much	36	85
	Disagree	61	15
	D.K.	3	0
		100	100
Big-business power	Too much	66	37
	Disagree	32	63
	D.K.	3	0
		101	100

large proportion of the men in our sample who are *both* trade union members and Labour Party voters would like to see the two wings of the Labour movement less closely associated. The exact figures are set out in table 15 which shows that only 55% of the Labour trade-unionists supported the present link between their party and the trade union movement.

This is not the place to present a detailed explanation of why such a large proportion of Labour voters and union members should favour the dissociation of political from industrial action. But on the basis of information we collected concerning their attitudes to work and their workplace behaviour we would argue that our sample of manual workers is characterised to a high degree by what we would call an 'instrumental' orientation towards their employment. That is to say, there is a marked tendency for our men to see not only their work and their relationships with their employers in a highly calculative manner,

TABLE 15. *Trade union support for Labour Party by union membership and by voting intention*

Voting intention	Union member	Trade union support for Labour Party			Total	N
		Approve	Keep separate	D.K.		
		Percentage				
Labour	Yes	55	43	2	100	141
	No	35	53	12	100	17
Conservative	Yes	19	81	0	100	21
	No	0	100	0	100	6

but also to adopt the same approach towards trade unionism. Union membership is important to them in order to help maximise their earnings in jobs that often provide few intrinsic rewards and offer negligible chances of individual advancement. But their style of trade unionism is very much an 'instrumental collectivism'. For them, the trade union is seen almost exclusively as a means of improving their standard of living, and not as an agency for transforming the social structure, or even as a way to greater worker participation in the affairs of the enterprise.[1]

It would appear, therefore, that although these affluent workers see the Labour Party as being closest to their interests as workers, they also take the view that trade unions exist for a specific and immediate purpose, and should confine themselves to making advances on the economic front instead of dissipating their resources in political activity.

Further evidence which goes to support this argument is the fact that only 50% of the trade unionists who were intending to vote Labour at the next election were knowingly paying their union's political levy. A further 27% were apparently paying the levy without being aware of it; but almost a quarter of the men who were both trade unionists and Labour supporters had 'contracted out'.[2] And even

[1] See Goldthorpe *et al.*, *The Affluent Worker: Industrial Attitudes and Behaviour*, chapter 5.
[2] Thus, 50% of the intending Labour voters claimed that they paid the political levy, 3% were unsure as to whether they paid or not, 14% claimed that they were not paying the levy but said that they had not 'contracted out', 10% claimed that they were paying the levy but did not know about 'contracting out', and 23% said that they did not pay the levy and had 'contracted out'.

among trade union members generally, leaving aside the question of political attachments, this would seem to be a relatively high proportion.[1]

It would thus appear that the strong contingent of Labour voters in our sample by no means wholly subscribes to the idea of a united Labour movement. Indeed, the tendency of a great many of these men to view politics and trade unionism as separate matters suggests that their attitudes are far removed from the 'solidaristic' left-wing outlook of Labour voters in more traditional working-class communities. In the concluding chapter of this monograph we shall seek to show how this difference in the quality of support for Labour is related to differences in the industrial and community *milieux* of the 'old' and the 'new' working class. For the time being, though, we simply note that the facts we have just presented do invite such a comparison.

The final aspect of our workers' political behaviour that we wish to consider concerns their everyday experience of political discussion and political influence. And this, too, has a bearing on differences in what we may call the 'primary' political environment of the traditional and the new industrial worker. In reply to the question: 'Within the past few weeks have you discussed political issues with anyone?' almost 60% of the manual sample replied in the negative. Of those who had discussed politics, over 80% had done so with their workmates, the remainder of the discussants being made up of friends, relatives, and trade union officers, in that order of importance.[2] It would seem then that 'politics' is not a very salient topic of conversation among our affluent workers, and although it cannot be demonstrated that they differ in this respect from more traditional workers, we would suspect that this is probably the case, if only because of the latter's higher participation in associations such as workingmen's clubs which, at the centre of the leisure-time activities of the traditional community, also provide a ready setting for informal talk about political issues.[3]

[1] See Martin Harrison, *Trade Unions and the Labour Party since 1945* (London, 1960), chapter 1.

[2] However, in case this should suggest that the workplace is a hive of political discussion, it should be noted that in our investigation of our workers' industrial behaviour it was found that the discussion of political issues formed but a very small proportion of the content of talk among workmates.

[3] Full details of our respondents' participation in associations will be given in forthcoming publications. But for preliminary findings, see Goldthorpe *et al.*, 'The Affluent Worker and the Thesis of *Embourgeoisement*'.

Furthermore, compared with the members of many kinds of more traditional working-class communities, the manual workers we studied were evidently much less exposed to a uniform pattern of personal influence, pushing them in the same political direction. Thus, in response to the question: 'Coming back to your friends, would you say that their political leanings are generally like yours, generally different, or mixed?', not more than 40% claimed that their friends shared their own political outlook. Almost 50% said that their friends were generally mixed in their political attitudes, and approximately one in ten claimed that their friends had political leanings which were generally different from their own.

Finally, it seems that the mass of our affluent workers do not feel themselves strongly oriented to any individuals whom they regard as opinion leaders. We asked: 'Is there anyone you know whose views on politics would carry a lot of weight with you?' 82% of the respondents could think of no one who fell into this category. The minority who did mention such 'political influentials' referred to relatives, friends, and trade union officers, in that order of importance.

On the basis of the replies to these three questions, then, it would seem that the primary groups to which our workers belong are in the main neither homogeneous in terms of political outlook nor important as sources of political influence and opinion.

We may now try to sum up the main points that have emerged in the course of the present chapter. Perhaps the most striking feature is that our sample of affluent manual workers, living in a town which has few of the characteristics of older industrial communities in the country, is nonetheless distinguished by its unusually strong and stable support for the Labour Party. In the General Elections of 1955 and 1959, no less than eight out of every ten votes that our workers cast for the three main parties were given to Labour; and the same proportion of intended votes went to Labour again at the time of our interviews in 1964. However, when we turn to examine the political orientations underlying this left-wing commitment, it would seem that our workers' attitudes are somewhat different from those of Labour's more traditional supporters among the working class. To be sure, the perception of the Labour Party as a 'class' party was very much in evidence in the replies given when our affluent workers were asked to account for their attachment to Labour. At the same time, though, in addition to these expressions of a diffuse sense of class loyalty, some of our men also took the view that the Labour Party commands their adherence because, by contrast with the other parties, it is the one which can do most for the ordinary working man in the way of increasing living standards and improving the social services. And, moreover, when the workers who intended to vote Labour at the next General Election were considering the significance of a possible Labour victory, they saw this largely in terms of the economic 'pay-offs' which might be expected from a Labour Government. The sober calculation of such material advantages is not, of course, incompatible with sentiments of 'class loyalty'. But other evidence that we collected does suggest that our affluent workers' support for Labour is probably less solidaristic and more instrumental than that of the many traditional workers from whom the Labour Party has in the past received almost unconditional allegiance. Thus, between a quarter and a third of the men in our sample who were intending to vote Labour did not feel that it would make a great deal of difference whether their party won the election or not. *Prima facie*, this might be taken to imply the opposite of what we are arguing, since despite their indifference these men were still in-tending to support Labour. But from the comments they made it is clear that their indifference to the outcome of the election was not associated with any great sense of solidarity with Labour, but was based rather on generally negative attitudes towards party politics in general. More significant than this fairly large element of the politically apathetic, however, are the facts that close to a half of intending Labour voters were not in favour of trade unions supporting the Labour Party and that a quarter of these same men had contracted out of paying their unions' political levy. The conclusion that may be drawn from these findings is that, in a very considerable number of cases, our workers' adherence to the Labour Party is regarded by them as being a quite separate issue from their membership of trade unions. To this extent, it would appear that there is at least a tendency for them to judge each of these organisations on its own merits rather than to accept, as a matter of course, that the industrial and political wings of the Labour movement should continue to work in such close association as has hitherto been the case. It is in this sense, then, that we would regard the political beliefs and values of the Labour voters in our sample as approximating what we have called an ideology of 'instrumental collectivism' by contrast with the 'solidaristic collectivism' of the traditional industrial worker. However, this element in our workers' political orientations must not be exaggerated; and the existence of more instrumental attitudes must not be taken to mean that Labour will not continue to have a strong base in the 'new' working class. This is an issue to which we shall return in the concluding chapter of the monograph. But first we wish to consider some further findings of our study which have a bearing on the familiar argument that growing prosperity has undermined support of the Labour Party among the more affluent section of the working class.

3. The politics of affluence

In this chapter our main concern will be with the thesis that working-class affluence leads, via a process of *embourgoisement*, to an erosion of Labour political loyalties. The circumstances which first lent force to this thesis are part of the familiar history of the 1950s and we need to refer to them here only briefly. Economically, these years were characterised by a relatively rapid rise in living standards and, most significantly perhaps, by a marked increase in the number of families achieving 'middle range' incomes.[1] This resulted in a considerable overlap, in terms of income, between those in manual and nonmanual occupations. Furthermore, important changes also occurred in the pattern of working-class consumption. Manual workers considerably increased their ownership of most kinds of durable consumer goods and for many items—such as TV sets, record players, washing machines and refrigerators—wide differences in the spread of ownership ceased to exist between the more prosperous manual and the lower white-collar strata. A sharp increase also occurred in the number of manual workers owning, or buying, their own homes and in the number possessing motor vehicles.

Politically, these years of growing prosperity were, of course, ones of undisputed Conservative dominance. In 1951 the Conservatives were returned to power with a majority of 26 over Labour; in 1955 they increased this figure to 67, and in 1959 raised it still higher to 107. These three successive victories, with rising majorities, were unparalleled in British electoral history. At the same time, the Labour vote showed signs of secular decline, falling from 49% of the total poll in 1951 to 46% in 1955 and to 44% in 1959. Moreover, there were indications that in those areas of the country which were economically the most progressive, this fall in the Labour vote was due to some significant extent to loss of support from among the industrial working class, either through defections or through new voters failing to follow in the traditional pattern.

In these circumstances, then, it can scarcely be regarded as surprising

[1] See John H. Goldthorpe and David Lockwood, 'Not So Bourgeois After All', *New Society*, vol. I, no. 3 (1962).

that the thesis of the progressive *embourgeoisement* of the British working class should have proved an attractive one. The argument that British society was becoming increasingly middle class provided a convenient means of linking together the outstanding economic and political developments of the period. It was, in fact, an argument accepted by spokesmen of both the right and left, by numerous journalists and social commentators, and by not a few political scientists and sociologists.[1] However, the existence of this general consensus of opinion did not alter the fact—though it may have served to obscure it—that the thesis of 'the worker turning middle class' lacked any satisfactory validation. It remained merely an assumption, or at best an inference, which it seemed reasonable to make in interpreting the socio-political situation in Britain at the end of the 1950s. Although the circumstantial evidence might be persuasive, very little direct evidence— and that of a relatively unsophisticated kind—could be presented to support the specific proposition that it was affluence *per se* that was chiefly responsible for the decline in the working-class Labour vote.

Perhaps the clearest statement of the 'affluence thesis' that has been made was that put forward by Butler and Rose in their study of the General Election of 1959. They begin with the observation that 'a significant number of skilled workers may be called class hybrids— working class in terms of occupation, education, speech and cultural norms, while being middle class in terms of income and material comforts'. They then go on to claim that those who are in this way 'on the threshold of the middle class are in some ways divided by conflict between their past and present, between their family and occupational traditions and their aspirations. They are thus exposed to conflicting political pressures. Voters subjected to such cross-pressures are particularly likely to abstain or to switch their voting allegiances.' According to this argument, then, a 'middle-class' standard of living produces a sense of social marginality; and this social marginality in turn leads to a lower Labour vote, either by way of abstention, or by way of a higher Conservative or Liberal vote. It is only fair to add that while Butler and Rose lay greatest stress on the workers' acquisition of a 'middle-class' standard of living, they also suggest that the effect of affluence will be more pronounced among those workers who have

[1] See the references given in Goldthorpe and Lockwood, 'Affluence and the British Class Structure' and in W. G. Runciman '*Embourgeoisement*, Self-rated Class and Party Preference,' *Sociological Review*, vol. 12, no. 2 (July 1964), p. 158 n. 8.

moved outside the sphere of influence of traditional working-class communities into new neighbourhoods, and who have developed new styles of consumption associated with a 'home-centred' existence.[1]

It may be noted that this account of the political consequences of *embourgeoisement* is rather more advanced than that which is involved in the familiar idea of the working-class 'prosperity voter'. The latter concept implies that erstwhile Labour supporters among the affluent working class are likely to become Conservative voters or to abstain from voting Labour as a direct result of their experience of rising standards of living under a Conservative Government. Thus the intermediate stage of social marginality that is postulated by Butler and Rose does not enter into this particular version of the affluence thesis. From the point of view of our study, however, the difference between the 'prosperity' and the 'social marginality' arguments is not especially significant. For the workers we studied were not only affluent but they tended to lead the relatively 'home-centred' lives that Butler and Rose regard as being conducive to a sense of social marginality.[2]

Although our research was not designed specifically to study the role of affluence as a factor leading to changes in political loyalties, our sample can provide a useful test of the affluence thesis, if only in an indirect way. In choosing our sample, our main consideration was, as we have noted, to select men whose earnings were clearly above the average for manufacturing industry as a whole, and whose take-home pay would compare favourably with that of lower white-collar workers. In this we were successful, as table 16 indicates. Thus 53% of the manual workers reported a take-home pay averaging more than £18 a week, whereas the proportion of white-collar workers who reported

[1] Butler and Rose, *The British General Election of 1959*, pp. 15–16. The authors do not mention other changes that may be associated with the 'new' working class and have rather different consequences for their social and political attitudes: namely, the tendency for such workers to be employed in large and heavily unionised plants, the declining possibilities of promotion from the shop floor, and, lastly, the re-housing of workers on new estates which are frequently just as 'one-class' in character as traditional working-class communities, if lacking the same degree of social integration as the latter. These issues will be taken up for further discussion in the concluding chapter of the monograph.

[2] This, as we have already explained in the Introduction, was part of the strategy of our research design; and the preliminary analysis of the data dealing with family and community life shows that in the main our workers did lead what we would term a relatively 'privatised' style of life. See Goldthorpe *et al.*, 'The Affluent Worker and the Thesis of *Embourgeoisement*', pp. 20–3. An account of our workers' perceptions of the class structure and of their own position in it will be presented in our final volume, which will also discuss the relationship between class imagery and voting behaviour.

35

more than this amount was only 38%. No doubt there are a fair number of manual workers who earn wages higher than the average received by our men. But since our main concern was with possible changes in social outlook and behaviour that could be held to be occurring on a relatively large scale our interest could not be centred on *exceptionally* high-earning groups. It is sufficient for our purposes that the men in our sample earned well above the average wages for men in manufacturing industry,[1] and that their wages are, on average, at least comparable with the earnings of the men in the white-collar sample.

When we turn to consider family incomes, it is true that there is a reversal in the relative earnings of the two groups. In the white-collar sample, 60% of families reported a total weekly income of more than £21 a week, whereas in the manual sample 50% fell into this category. This difference is accounted for by the higher proportion of working wives in the white-collar sample and this, in turn, may be related to the smaller family size of the white-collar group.[2] Finally, though, when

[1] A direct comparison of the earnings of the men in our manual sample with those of men in manufacturing industry is not possible, if only because our data for the former are reported earnings net of tax and other deductions whereas the figures given by the Ministry of Labour refer to gross earnings. A comparison is further complicated by the fact that the Ministry inquiry gives only a figure for mean earnings for years after 1960, although it notes that 'it is probable that the pattern of spread of earnings about the average has not altered significantly' in the later years. Working on this assumption, the following figures on the distribution of earnings for men in manufacturing industry in 1963 have been estimated by applying the increase in average earnings since 1960 to the whole distribution. See Ministry of Labour, *Statistics on Incomes, Prices, Employment and Production*, no. 17 (June 1966), table B. 14. We wish to thank Miss T. Seward of the Department of Applied Economics, University of Cambridge, for her help in making this calculation.

Average weekly earnings 1963

	Luton sample (men aged 21–46) after deductions £ s. d.	Men aged 21 and over in manufacturing industry before deductions £ s. d.
Mean	18 15 4	16 19 0
Median	18 7 0	16 16 0
Lower quartile	16 0 4	13 19 0
Upper quartile	20 11 5	20 5 0

[2] We are not suggesting that there is a direct causal relationship between small family size, on the one hand, and higher family income on the other. On the contrary, the fact that white-collar groups have both a small family size and high ratio of working wives may be explained as a result of the relatively high levels of aspiration and relatively low levels of

TABLE 16. *Income and possessions: manual and white-collar samples*

	Manual sample (N = 229) percentage	White-collar sample (N = 54) percentage
Income		
Reported average weekly earnings *net* of tax, etc. i.e., 'take-home pay'		
Husband:		
Under £18	47	61
£18 and over	53	38
	100[a]	99[b]
Family:		
Under £21	50	40
£21 and over	50	60
	100[a]	100[b]
Possessions		
Percentage owning:		
House	57	69
Car	45	52
Refrigerator	57	56
Telephone	7	17

[a] One respondent declined to answer.
[b] Two respondents declined to answer.

we compare the two samples with respect to home-ownership and possession of durable consumer goods, we see that while the white-collar group are rather more likely to own houses and cars than the manual group, the differences in ownership are not on the whole very great.

We may conclude, therefore, that manual workers in our sample are clearly very well-off relative to manual workers generally, and that they enjoy what may be regarded as a 'lower middle-class' standard of living, roughly comparable with that of our sample of white-collar workers.

income among this 'status marginal' section of the lower middle class. This suggests that, although our sample of manual workers are rather better off than the white-collar sample as far as husbands earnings are concerned, their family's level of aspiration for status and/ or possessions is probably lower than that of the white-collar group. If this is so, it may imply that the manual group are on the whole relatively more satisfied with their economic and/or social status and thus do not possess, to the same degree, the 'lower middle-class' aspirations of the white-collar worker.

37

The affluent worker: political attitudes

If the affluence thesis is correct, then it ought to follow that these manual workers should be clearly less left-wing in their political sympathies than are manual workers in the country at large. However, as we have already seen, this conclusion is not supported by our data. Despite the fact that the men in our sample undoubtedly earn higher wages, are more often house-owners, and have more durable consumer goods than the majority of manual workers, they also register a notably high and solid Labour vote.

This general conclusion is, of course, open to the possible objection that the sample of manual workers we chose was not 'sufficiently affluent' to test the affluence thesis properly. To this, we would reply, first, that in terms of the thesis itself our workers should clearly qualify as a critical sample since they can be shown to be enjoying at least a 'lower middle-class standard of living'; and secondly, that, if by this measure their standard of living is not regarded as 'middle class' enough, the burden of proof lies with the affluence theorists, who must specify the exact level of affluence that is needed to produce the results that they postulate. It is also worth making the obvious point that the difference in support for Labour between our manual and white-collar samples cannot be readily interpreted in terms of their relative economic conditions. It might conceivably be argued, of course, that the role of affluence is not something that operates 'across the board' but is only important among manual workers. However, here again, it could be said that the exponents of the affluence thesis have never in fact specified this limitation; and in terms of the underlying logic of the thesis it is not clear why it should exist.

The fact that the workers in our sample exhibit overall a relatively high Labour vote may, then, be regarded as at all events highly inconsistent with any unqualified affluence thesis. However, within the sample it is of course possible to distinguish between men who are, so to speak, more or less affluent than others. By dividing up our sample in terms of such factors as income and house-ownership we can therefore test the affluence thesis further; and we can in this way partly take into account the possible objection that the men who fell into our sample were 'not affluent enough' to constitute a proper test of this thesis.

As can be seen from table 17, differences in family income have almost no effect on Labour voting, but differences in husband's earnings produce a slightly lower intended Labour vote among the

TABLE 17. *Voting intention by income*

				Voting intention			
	Lab.	Cons.	Lib.	Uncertain (incline to Lib. or abstain)	Abstain	Total	Nᵃ
				Percentage			
Husband's earnings							
Less than £18	79	12	5	0	3	99	96
£18 or more	74	14	8	2	3	101	110
Family income							
Less than £21	77	10	6	2	5	100	103
£21 or more	75	16	8	0	1	100	103

ᵃ N = 206. See note ᶜ, table 3 and note ᵃ, table 16.

higher income group.[1] While the latter finding could be constructed as evidence in favour of the affluence thesis, the effect is not very marked; and from the point of view of this thesis it is in any case not entirely obvious why it should be the husband's rather than the family income which affects Labour voting. And, even if we isolate a particularly affluent group—men earning more than £21 a week— table 18 shows that still no very marked decrease in Labour voting is produced.

The association between house-ownership and vote is presented in table 19. Here it is at once apparent that the affluence thesis is supported by the fact that house-owners are less prone to vote Labour than are men living in council houses and other rented accommodation. Nevertheless, the differences in intended Labour voting are again not

[1] Since our data on income and house-ownership refer to our respondents' economic situation at the time of the study, the following tables relate differences in level of affluence to our respondents' voting intentions. However, it may be said that cross-tabulations substituting voting in the General Election of 1959 for voting intention produced very similar results. This reflects the fact of the high degre of stability in the voting behaviour of our sample (table 8 above). It should also be noted that in all subsequent tables relating to voting intention, the 16 men in the sample whose voting intention was 'don't know' have been excluded, so that unless otherwise indicated the total size of the sample is reduced from 223 to 207. In fact, the inclusion or the exclusion of the 'don't knows' does not materially affect any of the conclusions that are reached. Following the argument of Butler and Rose, however, we have included abstaining as a possible form of 'non-Labour voting'.

TABLE. 18 *Voting intention by husband's earnings*

| | Voting intention | | | | | | |
	Lab.	Cons.	Lib.	Uncertain (incline to Lib. or abstain)	Abstain	Total	N[a]
			Percentage				
Husband's earnings							
Less than £18	79	12	5	0	3	99	96
£18 or more but less than £21	74	11	7	3	4	99	70
£21 or more	73	17	10	0	0	100	40

[a] N = 206. See note [a], table 17.

great, being in fact of much the same order as those associated with differences in husband's earnings.

However, if we combine income and house-ownership as in table 20 it can be seen that the differences in voting intention between the most and least 'affluent' of our workers becomes rather more pronounced. The house-owners earning more than £18 a week have an intended Labour vote of 73%, while for men earning less than this amount, and not owning their own houses, the figure rises to 82%.

These findings are certainly consistent with the affluence thesis. However, it is the specific claim of this thesis that it is the loyalty of the Labour supporter that is strained by the fact of his prosperity. Therefore, it is of some interest to see whether the relationship between affluence and intended voting just noted also holds among those men in our sample who voted for Labour in the election of 1959. In table 21 we make this comparison between the voting intentions of 1959 Labour voters of greater and lesser affluence, as measured by husband's earnings and house-ownership. From this table, it is clear that there is no systematic relationship between level of affluence and stability of Labour voting. Thus, the most affluent group propose to give 93% of their votes to the Labour Party, while for the least affluent group the figure is 95%. Since there can be no question that the former group of workers have attained, if not surpassed, the level of income and material comfort enjoyed by a great many employees in the white-collar middle class, the fact that these affluent workers show no

40

TABLE 19. *Voting intention by house-ownership*

	Voting intention						
	Lab.	Cons.	Lib.	Uncertain (incline to Lib. or abstain)	Abstain	Total	Nᵃ
	Percentage						
House-owner	74	13	9	1	3	100	119
Other	80	13	3	1	3	100	88

ᵃ N = 207. See note ᶜ, table 3.

TABLE 20. *Voting intention by husband's earnings and by house-ownership*

	Voting intention						
	Lab.	Cons.	Lib.	Uncertain (incline to Lib. or abstain)	Abstain	Total	Nᵃ
	Percentage						
Husband's earnings:							
£18 or more							
House-owner	73	14	9	1	3	100	74
Other	75	14	6	3	3	101	36
Less than £18							
House-owner	76	13	9	0	2	100	45
Other	82	12	2	0	4	100	51

ᵃ N = 206. See note ᵃ, table 17.

particular tendency to abandon their support of Labour is inconsistent with what the affluence thesis would predict.[1]

Yet another possible way of testing the argument that prosperity is a force weakening working-class support for Labour is to compare the voting behaviour of men who have always lived in Luton with that of

[1] It appears also inconsistent with the finding of table 20 that a relationship is to be found between level of affluence and level of Labour voting. But as we shall see in the following chapter, this relationship is in fact largely capable of being 'explained away' by the introduction of a third variable: namely, the extensiveness of a worker's 'white-collar affiliations'. When the latter is controlled for, the relationship between level of affluence and level of Labour voting almost disappears. See below, pp. 56-9.

TABLE 21. *Voting intentions of Labour voters of 1959 by husband's earnings and by house-ownership*

Labour voters of 1959	Voting intention						
	Lab.	Cons.	Lib.	Uncertain (incline to Lib. or abstain)	Abstain	Total	N[a]
	Percentage						
Husband's earnings:							
Less than £18							
House-owner	88	3	6	0	3	100	33
Other	95	2	2	0	0	99	40
£18 or more							
House-owner	93	2	4	0	0	99	45
Other	100	0	0	0	0	100	24

[a] N = 142. See table 8 and note [a], table 16. There were five respondents who were unsure about their voting intention.

men who have been attracted to Luton from other parts of the country. We have good reason to believe that those men in our sample who migrated to Luton did so in the majority of cases because of the lure of higher wages and better housing.[1] Therefore, if the migrants have comparable incomes and possessions to the 'native' Lutonians, the former group might be expected in the main to have experienced a greater relative improvement in their standard of living than the latter group. And since in the last resort the undermining of Labour loyalties that is postulated by the affluence thesis must result from the worker's own perception of his improved standard of living, the migrants should have a lower propensity to vote Labour than the 'native' Lutonians.

In table 22 we compare the voting intentions of these two groups, holding constant level of affluence as measured by husband's earnings and house-ownership. We see that in every case except that of the least affluent workers the migrants intended to give a higher proportion of their votes to the Labour Party than did the men who had always lived in Luton. Thus, for example, 75% of the most affluent migrants intended to vote for the Labour Party as opposed to 68% of the comparable group of native Lutonians. Moreover, differences in level of

See chapter 1, p. 9, above.

TABLE 22. *Voting intention by husband's area of upbringing, by husband's earnings and by house-ownership*

Husband's area of upbringing	Husband's earnings	House-owner	Voting intention							
			Lab.	Cons.	Lib.	Uncertain (incline to Lib. or abstain)	Abstain	Total	Nᵃ
			Percentage							
Lutonians	£18 or more	Yes	68	16	10	0	5	99	19
		No	67	33	0	0	0	100	9
	Less than £18	Yes	68	16	10	0	5	99	19
		No	82	12	6	0	0	100	17
Migrants	£18 or more	Yes	75	13	9	2	2	101	55
		No	78	7	7	4	4	100	27
	· Less than £18	Yes	80	12	8	0	0	100	25
		No	81	12	0	0	6	99	32

ᵃ N = 203. See note ᵃ, table 17. No information on area of upbringing was available for four respondents; and one of these respondents was also still ineligible to vote.

affluence would appear to have less effect upon voting among the migrant workers, even though from the point of view of the argument under consideration one might expect just the opposite. Yet while there is a difference of only five percentage points between the proportions voting Labour in the most and the least affluent groups of migrants the corresponding figure for the comparable Lutonian groups is fourteen percentage points.

Any conclusion that we may draw from these data is bound to be highly tentative. But we can at least say that those workers in our sample who have been attracted to Luton by the prospect of a higher standard of living, and who have actually succeeded in finding it, are not less likely to support the Labour Party than the workers who have not had to move house and home in search of prosperity. The fact that a higher proportion of migrants than Lutonians intended to vote for the Labour Party does not, of course, demonstrate that the proportion of Labour supporters among the migrant group—and especially among the most affluent migrants—has not declined by comparison with what it was before they moved to Luton. On this point, our data can provide no conclusive answer. But in the voting histories of the most affluent migrant workers there is no indication of any marked swing

4-2

away from voting Labour to voting Conservative, Liberal or abstaining. On the contrary, the proportion voting for the Labour Party seems to have been remarkably stable.[1] Migration, whatever its effects on other aspects of our workers' lives, does not seem to have had any noticeable consequences for their political allegiances; even among the men who have crossed the threshold of a 'lower middle-class' standard of living.

A final test of the affluence thesis can be attempted by examining the relationship between voting and our workers' own estimates of the changes in their living standards. We asked our respondents: 'Would you say that over the past ten years your standard of living has gone up, or down, or stayed about the same?' This question was followed by another which asked: 'Well, comparing yourself with other people, would you say that you have done better than they have, worse, or about the same?' In this way, we obtained measures of our workers' perceptions of their 'prosperity' relative to both their own previous positions and those of others.[2] The response to these questions provides us with data that are highly relevant to the argument being considered because, unless the worker feels that he is affluent, especially by comparison with other manual workers, he is unlikely to start thinking of himself as potentially 'middle class' in the way that is assumed by the affluence thesis.

In answer to the first question 78% of the sample thought that their standard of living had gone up; 19% thought that it was more or less the same; and 3% believed that they were now worse off than they had been ten years ago. On the whole, then, our workers' subjective estimates of changes in their standards of living are in line with what on the basis of their objective position as earners and consumers we should expect them to be.

[1] We recorded all changes in voting, including changes from voting for a particular party to abstaining and *vice versa*, for all our respondents from the General Election of 1945 to the election of 1959 inclusive. Among the most affluent migrant workers there were 16 such changes in voting: two of these involved a change from voting Labour to voting Conservative (1) or Liberal (1); and three involved a change from voting Conservative to voting Labour (2) or abstaining (1). It may also be noted that at the General Election of 1955—some eight years prior to the time of our research—71% of those eligible to vote among the most affluent immigrants gave their vote to Labour as opposed to voting Conservative, Liberal or abstaining. From table 22 above it will be seen that the corresponding figure for voting intention is 75%.

[2] These two questions were designed to lead on to a third: 'Who is it that you're thinking of when you say that you've done (better) (worse) (the same)?' This last question was aimed at discovering the actual reference groups of our respondents in their role as consumers. The results of this analysis will be reported elsewhere. Here it may simply be noted that their reference groups were overwhelmingly people in the same class as themselves—neighbours, workmates, friends, and relatives.

44

TABLE 23. *Voting intention by evaluation of change in standard of living*

Standard of living		Voting intention						
Change over last ten years	Compared with 'other' people	Lab.	Cons.	Lib.	Uncertain (incline to Lib. or abstain)	Abstain	Total	N
		Percentage						
Up	Better	74	11	7	2	7	101	61
Up	Same	76	14	8	1	1	100	93
Same	Same	80	12	8	0	0	100	25

When comparing their own living standards with those of 'other people' they were, however, less optimistic: 35% thought that they had done better than others as against 61% who judged that they had done equally well. On the other hand, though, only 2% considered that they had done worse, while a further 2% were unable to make the comparison.

As a result of correlating our respondents' replies to these two questions we find that the large majority of the sample (87%) fall into three main groups: (i) those who thought that their standard of living had risen and who also thought that they had done better than others; (ii) those who thought that their standard of living had risen but not appreciably more than that of other people; and (iii) those who thought that they were more or less in the same position as before and had done neither better nor worse than other people. The first group—the self-rated 'achievers'—were a sizable minority, and indeed by objective measures of house-ownership and husband's earnings they were in fact relatively more affluent than the other two groups. If the affluence thesis is correct, it is this particular group of workers in our sample that should be least committed to the Labour Party. As may be seen from table 23, they do actually have the lowest intended Labour vote. But it should be noted that this is only fractionally less than the proportion of votes intended for the Labour Party in the second group, and not very much lower than the Labour vote of the third group, that is, of the men who were not very impressed by what they had gained as consumers. Although these findings are in line with the affluence thesis, they can hardly be regarded as constituting a very powerful confirmation of it. Moreover, when we take into account *both* objective measures and subjective estimates of standard of living a very different result is obtained. If we single out those of our respondents who not only felt themselves to be comparatively well off but who were also among the most affluent in that they owned their own houses and earned £18 or more a week, we then find that 81 % of this group intended to vote for the Labour Party at the next General Election.[1] This particular piece of evidence cannot of course be regarded as a conclusive refutation of the affluence thesis, but it is nevertheless a striking fact that the workers who were most affluent *and* relatively most satisfied with the improvement in their standard of living over the last ten years were also considerably more pro-Labour than the sample as a whole.

As we have said at the beginning of this chapter, our study does not allow us to make as thorough an investigation of the effects of affluence on voting as would be desirable to test the affluence thesis decisively. We have noted that this thesis itself is in some respects imprecise, and would need clarification and refinement in order to be tested in any definitive way. However, since we ourselves do not embrace it, we shall leave this task to those who do. We have seen that, as a result of the various analyses we have made, some—albeit slight—evidence can be produced that is consistent with the thesis as we have interpreted it. In the case of the workers we studied, there is some relationship between particularly high earnings and house-ownership, on the one hand, and the likelihood of not voting Labour on the other. By far the strongest differentiation in Labour voting was produced by a measure of affluence that combined husband's earnings and house-ownership. At the same time, though, differences in family income, geographical mobility, and subjective estimates of changes in standard of living appear to have no very great effect so far as party allegiance is concerned.

Moreover, in this respect we must not lose sight of the basic fact that even the most affluent group within our sample—men earning £18 or more a week take-home pay and owning their own houses—still registers a high Labour vote relative to manual workers in the country at large. If we consider the votes which this most affluent group had prospectively committed to the three main parties in 1963–4, we find

[1] The number of respondents falling into this category was twenty-six; the rest of their intended votes were distributed as follows: Conservative Party, 8%; Liberal Party, 8%; abstain, 4%.

that no fewer than 75% were intending to support the Labour Party. This then brings us back to the main finding with which we started: namely that our sample as a whole, while clearly affluent by comparison with lower white-collar and other manual workers, is strong and stable in its allegiance to Labour, as indicated both by voting history and by voting intention at the time of our interviews. So far as politics is concerned, this is the most important conclusion of our study and it provides no backing at all for those who claim that affluence is incompatible with a continuing high level of support for Labour among the industrial labour force.

Finally, before leaving our discussion of the affluence thesis, we would like to draw attention to what we believe to be its shortcomings from a theoretical point of view. The major flaw in the thesis, in our view, lies in the assumption that a certain level of income and possessions (itself never clearly specified) leads to a feeling of social marginality among manual workers. But why, one may ask, should this be so? Neither actual membership nor an aspiration to membership in social, as opposed to statistical, groups is an automatic consequence of having a certain level of income and possessions. Therefore, since individuals do not develop orientations or attachments to abstract statistical collectivities, such as the 'middle income bracket', it is difficult to see in what sense an affluent worker is cross-pressured between his 'middle-class standard of living' and his role as a manual wage-earner. To be sure, the latter role does involve him in social relationships which lead to characteristic experiences and attitudes which differ from those, say, of men who are salaried nonmanual employees. In this sense, being a manual worker does orient the individual towards actual collectivities which from his point of view may be either 'membership' groups or 'reference' groups or both. But a certain standard of living, measured simply by income and possessions, does not likewise result in any direct way either in participation in different membership groups or in the adoption of reference groups other than those which derive from his role as a manual wage-earner. Being affluent does not mean that the worker becomes a member of middle-class society or even aspires to such membership. To take one obvious example: no amount of relative affluence in the past appears to have led to any diminution of class solidarity in communities of mine-workers, even though class feeling may have become weaker in these communities of late as a result of changes which are the concomitants of

47

growing prosperity. In brief, then, the confusion in the affluence thesis stems basically from the ambiguous phrase 'middle-class standard of living', which merely begs the question of whether such a standard of living makes a family middle class in any social, as opposed to a statistical, sense. The auxiliary hypothesis that affluence is only a necessary, but not a sufficient, condition for the development of middle-class aspirations and the worker's assimilation into middle-class society, is, of course, more plausible. But this qualified affluence thesis is even more vague than the original one because it lacks specification of the other factors involved in such a process of *embourgeoisement*, and it still makes the questionable assumption that, given these other factors, affluence remains a highly relevant consideration.

Our own view is that the role of affluence in working-class politics, even as a necessary condition of non-Labour voting, has still to be proven. A worker's prosperity, or lack of it, is only one element entering into the formation of his class and political awareness; and, when compared with the experiences and influences to which he is daily exposed at his place of work, in his local community, and within his own family circle, the effect of such purely material factors as level of income and possessions may well be a relatively minor one. The weakness of the affluence thesis is that it fails to take account of the worker's social relationships, and particularly of the way in which they affect the *meaning* which the individual worker places on the fact of his prosperity or privation. Indeed, the role of these social factors may be so strong as to override considerations of affluence altogether. For, even though it may be possible to find some degree of association between affluence and voting, it may still be the case that, if one controls for other, more theoretically relevant factors, this association no longer exists. In the next chapter, we shall follow up this line of argument by examining the effects on voting of two salient aspects of our workers' group attachments: namely, the extensiveness of their 'white-collar affiliations' and their trade union membership.

4. Politics and group affiliations

A number of studies have by now demonstrated that the inculcation, maintenance and change of political loyalties are, under normal circumstances, mainly attributable to the effects of the personal influences to which individuals are exposed at different stages of their lives. The family is the most important initial agency of socialisation into partisanship; and this attachment to party is, in the majority of cases, reinforced by the cumulative impact of later experiences which the individual encounters in his work and community relationships.[1] Later influences are generally reinforcing because in most instances the individual occupies a position in the social order which is broadly comparable with that of his parents. Social mobility does occur, however, and here research has shown that changes in voting behaviour or voting behaviour which is 'deviant' in terms of the individual's current class position are due in some large measure to the influences to which he has been exposed as result of inter- or intragenerational mobility.[2]

Class position, even if broadly conceived, is not, of course, the only aspect of group membership which affects voting. But in Great Britain, a society which is to a large degree ethnically and religiously homogeneous, there are few lines of cleavage, other than those of class, which divide the population decisively in terms of politics.[3] In this chapter, therefore, we shall concentrate on differences in our affluent workers' experience of class and status; differences of a kind which are known to be related to variations in the level of working-class support for the Labour Party.

There are two main aspects which our data allow us to analyse. First, there are differences arising from the social origins and occupational careers of our respondents and their wives. These differences will be examined from the point of view of the number of affiliations that our

[1] See H. H. Hyman, *Political Socialization* (Glencoe, 1959).
[2] Thus, for example, it has been pointed out that 'the results of voting studies in five countries provide considerable support for the hypothesis that downward mobile persons are less likely to identify with the political and economic organisations of the working class than manual workers who inherit their class status': S. M. Lipset and Reinhard Bendix, *Social Mobility in Industrial Society* (Berkeley, 1959), pp. 69-70.
[3] The best discussion of the saliency of 'class politics' in Great Britain is by Alford, *Party aud Society*, chapter 6.

49

workers have, or have had, with people who might be regarded as 'middle class', that is, people with white-collar occupational status. To put it in a slightly different way, we shall be looking at the extent to which our respondents are likely to have been exposed to middle-class personal influence. For workers in traditional working-class communities, the amount of past or present affiliation with members of white-collar strata is usually very small. In these communities, manual workers tend overwhelmingly to be the sons of manual workers, and, because of the predominantly 'one-class' nature of the localities in which they live and work, their contact with white-collar persons outside the family group is also likely to be relatively slight. By contrast, in more occupationally heterogeneous communities, the amount of contact between persons of blue-collar and white-collar status will be correspondingly greater.

In our own research, we deliberately chose a community that had a fairly well-balanced occupational structure and one in which manual workers tended not to live in isolated working-class enclaves. We find, in fact, that within our sample, there is a relatively high proportion of men who have either come from white-collar homes themselves (20%) or who have white-collar fathers-in-law (24%); and an even greater proportion have married wives who have had, or currently hold, white-collar jobs (45%). Finally, a certain number of our affluent workers have themselves spent some of their working lives in white-collar employment (10%).[1] From this point of view, our sample is characterised, to a higher degree than would probably be the case with a sample of more traditional workers, by numerous 'family bridges' with the world of the middle class.[2]

[1] In fact these several attributes are not highly correlated, which means that only a minority of the men in our sample (31%) are without any such kind of white-collar affiliation. See table 24 below; also Goldthorpe *et al.*, *The Affluent Worker: Industrial Attitudes and Behaviour*, pp. 155–7.

[2] One other aspect of inter-class influence is the degree to which manual workers have friends, as opposed to relatives, in white-collar occupations. We should expect to find that in the main those men who have family and occupational 'bridges' with the middle class would also tend to be the men whose friends (other than relatives) are more likely to include white-collar persons. This is probable because white-collar friends are likely to be acquired more readily through one's relatives or through contacts at one's place of work. In fact, the data we have so far analysed show that there is this sort of relationship within our sample, the men with the most family and occupational affiliations with the middle class having the most white-collar friends. It has been suggested by Blau that, in addition to a worker's experience of social mobility, the extensiveness of his middle-class friendships will have a quite independent influence on his voting behaviour. See Peter M. Blau, 'Social Mobility and Interpersonal Relations', *American Sociological Review*, vol. 19

A second major respect in which the class situation of our workers differs from that of some other manual employees is that they all work in large-scale plants and are fairly heavily unionised. In this they differ not so much from traditional workers of the 'proletarian' variety, who are employed in such industries as mining, docking, shipbuilding, and heavy metals, as from the other variety of traditional worker, the 'deferential', who is more likely to be found working in small-scale enterprises where he is usually in a relatively close personal relationship with his employer and less subject to trade union influences. It is known that an association tends to exist between size of work organisation, degree of unionisation, and left-wing voting.[1] The causal nexus is probably complex. First, trade unions are more likely to devote their organising efforts to larger plants where workers are conveniently concentrated. Secondly, the more routinised and disciplined nature of work in large plants, the physical and symbolic segregation of manual from nonmanual employees, the collective pressure of workmate opinion, and the probability that unsatisfying jobs make the extrinsic rewards of pay and conditions very prominent in the worker's mind are all factors which predispose workers in large plants to join trade unions. Finally, given the existence of strong trade union organisation, the political pressure that is applied by union officials and the more active rank-and-file members, especially at times of General Elections, will be more likely to produce a high Labour vote than in situations where this organisation is weak or lacking altogether. But whatever the nature of the entire causal chain involved, we should certainly expect to find that there is a significant difference in support for Labour between the unionised and non-unionised men in our sample.

We consider first the facts on white-collar affiliation, and here we have two sets of information at our disposal: the occupations of the respondent's father and father-in-law; and a complete record of the main[2] occupations held by the respondent and his wife. The detailed classification that was used to analyse data on social origin and job history is set out in appendix D. For most purposes this detailed classification was collapsed so as to produce three main occupational status categories: white-collar, intermediate, and manual. In the fol-

(1954), pp. 175–85. Our data are not yet ready enough to test Blau's hypothesis. We intend to discuss it in a later publication.
[1] S. M. Lipset, *Political Man* (London, 1960) pp. 249–50.
[2] I.e. those held for one year or more.

TABLE 24. *Conjugal white-collar affiliations*

Social origins	Job history	N^a	Conjugal white-collar affiliations (family and job)
Husband's and/or wife's father *white collar*	Husband's and/or wife's highest job *white collar*	57	Both
Husband's and/or wife's father *white collar*	Husband's and wife's highest job *intermediate* or *manual*	31	Family only
Husband's and wife's father *intermediate* or *manual*	Husband's and/or wife's highest job *white collar*	70	Job only
Husband's and wife's father *intermediate* or *manual*	Husband's and wife's highest job *intermediate* or *manual*	70	Neither

[a] N = 228. No information on social origins was available for one respondent.

owing discussion this trichotomous scale has been further simplified and the operative distinction is between white-collar occupations, on the one hand, and intermediate and manual occupations on the other. Using this dichotomous classification, data on the social origins and job history of husband and wife were combined to produce a measure of 'conjugal white-collar affiliations'. How this was done should be clear from table 24. Thus, for example, those men whose fathers and/or fathers-in-law held white-collar jobs and who themselves and/or their wives had ever held white-collar jobs, were placed in the top category; while, in contrast, if neither spouse came from a white-collar home or had ever held a white-collar job, the respondent was placed in the bottom category.

This form of classification was adopted for both theoretical and practical reasons. Since class position, usually measured by occupation, seems to exert such a strong influence not only on voting but on other forms of social behaviour, it would seem worthwhile to explore some of its other dimensions than just that of the currently held job of the respondent. In particular, it would seem profitable to consider the total number of primary white-collar affiliations that a manual worker has, or has had, as a member of a conjugal unit.[1] In other words, we assume

[1] Cf. Angus Campbell, Philip E. Converse, Warren E. Miller and Donald E. Stokes, *The American Voter* (New York, 1960), p. 376: 'Even a relatively remote factor such as a wife's father's occupational status exerts a visible pull that, when discrepant with a

that the jobs held by the individual's father and father-in-law, and his wife's present or past job, as well as his own previous jobs, will have a marked and cumulative effect in differentiating attitudes and behaviour among men whose present jobs are manual. We would expect that manual workers whose white-collar affiiliations are extensive will be more prone to adopt middle-class attitudes and forms of behaviour, including political ones, than the manual workers who are completely lacking in such affiliations. The reason for expecting this to be so is that, other things being equal, the likelihood of exposure to middle-class norms and middle-class personal influence will of course be far greater in the former case than in the latter.

From a practical point of view, the particular classification used is also convenient because of the small size of our sample. As may be seen from table 24, the sample divides itself on this basis into four categories, each of which is large enough to permit some degree of breakdown against other variables. We should, of course, have liked to be able to use an even finer classification, and the present one is in fact asymmetrical in that the bottom group (the men having neither family nor job affiliations) is more 'purely' manual in character than the top category (the men having some family and job affiliations) is 'purely' white collar. To correct this asymmetry isolate, it would have been necessary to a category of men whose fathers and fathers-in-law were both in white-collar occupations *and* whose own *as well as* their wives' job histories included white-collar employment. However, while in principle this group would have been a most interesting one to study, in practice it would have been too small to permit useful analysis.

The present classification is, then, meaningful in terms of what we know about social mobility and is also one that can be effectively applied to the data we have at our disposal.[1] Nevertheless, it has two shortcomings which must simply be noted. It is incomplete because it does not exhaust the entire range of social relationship through which manual workers may be exposed to white-collar influence. And it is crude in that it does not take into account the relative length of time during which spouses were employed in white-collar as opposed to manual work, and also because it assumes that the affiliations of

man's current status, increases the probability of mis-identification.' Mis-identification is defined as the discrepancy between objective occupational position and self-estimated status.

[1] As far as we know, this particular breakdown has not been used in previous studies, although a very similar one has been put to effective use in the investigation of educational achievement. See J. W. B. Douglas, *The Home and the School* (London, 1965), pp. 41-9.

parentage and of job are of equivalent importance and simply additive. This latter assumption in fact makes it desirable to simplify the classification set out in table 24 even further by collapsing the two intermediate categories and treating them as one. For since we have no theoretical grounds for predicting voting differences between men who have *only* family or *only* job affiliations, it is obviously advisable to bring these respondents together in the same group. Thus, in all subsequent tables, individuals are classified as to the extent of their white-collar affiliations in a threefold way: that is, as having 'both', 'either' or 'neither' of the two types of affiliations that are in question.

The relationship between the degree of white-collar affiliation and voting in the General Election of 1959 is presented in table 25. It can be seen that there is a marked difference in Labour voting between the workers who have white-collar affiliations through both family and occupation[1] and the workers who have neither type of affiliation. This breakdown of the sample, it should be emphasised, produces a far stronger differentiation in the level of Labour voting than any that was obtained by dividing up the sample in terms of income, house-ownership, or indeed any other of the variables connected with the 'affluence thesis'. Moreover, although table 25 refers only to the election of 1959, the same pattern is clearly evident if we analyse our respondents' voting histories from 1945 onwards, and, as will be seen later, a similar distribution again occurs when we take voting intentions at the time of the interviews in 1963–4.[2]

An exactly comparable breakdown is not possible in the case of our white-collar sample because there were too few respondents who had ever occupied manual jobs in the course of their careers. We can, however, divide the nonmanual workers in terms of conjugal social origins alone. When this is done, it will be seen from table 26 that those men of lower social origins gave 39% of their votes to the

---

[1] Strictly speaking, we should refer to a worker's *conjugal* white-collar affiliations. But this seemed excessively cumbersome. However, it should be remembered that it is *possible* for a respondent to be classified as having 'both' family and occupational affiliations simply by virtue of his being married to a woman who is 'white collar' in social origin and who has also held a 'white-collar' job.

[2] It may also be noted that, among those workers who were 'attached' to the Labour Party, the men who had both family and occupational affiliations of a white-collar kind were less likely than were the men having neither type of white-collar affiliation to: (i) identify the Labour Party as the party of the 'working class' or 'working man' (45% as opposed to 65%); and (ii) approve of trade union support of the Labour Party (45% as opposed to 56%).

TABLE 25. *Vote in General Election 1959 by conjugal white-collar affiliations: manual sample*

Conjugal white-collar affiliations (family and job)	Vote in General Election 1959					Total	N[a]
	Lab.	Cons.	Lib.	Abstain	D.K.		
	Percentage						
Both	59	24	6	11	0	100	54
Either	71	13	4	12	0	100	93
Neither	81	10	0	10	0	101	63

[a] N = 210. See note [b], table 3, and note [a], table 24.

TABLE 26. *Vote in General Election 1959 by social origin of husband and wife: white-collar sample*

Special Origin	Vote in General Election 1959					Total	N[a]
	Lab.	Cons.	Lib.	Abstain	D.K.		
	Percentage						
Husband's and/or wife's father *white collar*	15	63	18	4	0	100	27
Husband's and wife's fathers *intermediate* or *manual*	39	44	9	9	0	101	23

[a] N = 50. See note [e], table 3.

Labour Party in 1959, as opposed to a figure of 15% for those of higher social origins. This difference in the proportions of Labour supporters within the two nonmanual groups (24%) is, in fact, greater than that between manual workers with both types of white-collar affiliation and manual workers with neither type of affiliation (22%); it is also greater than that between nonmanual workers of lower social origin and manual workers with both types of white-collar affiliations (20%). Thus it is apparent that if we control for degree of white-collar affiliation there is no longer any sharp discontinuity in partisanship between our manual and nonmanual samples. As far as Labour voting is concerned, manual workers of 'middle-class' backgrounds have as much in common with nonmanual workers of 'working-class' backgrounds as they have with manual workers of 'working-class' backgrounds. And, conversely, nonmanual workers of 'working-class' backgrounds have

55

TABLE 27. *Husband's earnings and house-ownership by conjugal white-collar affiliations*

| Conjugal white-collar affiliations (family and job) | Husband's average weekly earnings | | | | | | Percentage earning £18 or more | Percentage owning own house |
| | £18 or more | | Less than £18 | | Total | Nᵃ | | |
	Own house	other	Own house	Other				
	Percentage							
Both	42	18	19	21	100	57	60	61
Either	40	14	28	19	101	101	54	68
Neither	25	23	14	38	100	69	48	39

ᵃ N = 227. See note ᵃ, table 16 and note ᵃ, table 24.

as much in common with manual workers of 'middle-class' backgrounds as they have with nonmanual workers of 'middle-class' backgrounds.

In the last chapter it was shown that within our sample of manual workers there was a definite, though not very strong, relationship between affluence and voting. We have just seen that by dividing our sample in terms of respondents' white-collar affiliations an even more marked difference in voting patterns can be obtained. We can now show that there is an association between white-collar affiliation and affluence in that those workers with neither family nor occupational ties with the middle class are less affluent than workers with both or either one of these ties. Table 27 shows that 61% of the men with both types, as opposed to only 39% of those with neither type, of affiliation were house-owners; and that whereas 60% of those in the former category earned more than £18 a week, this was true only of 48% of those in the latter category. The meaning of this difference, which we do not believe is accidental, will be discussed elsewhere. For the time being, it will simply be treated as a datum.

Given that in our sample being 'more affluent' is associated with having white-collar affiliations, and given also that both these characteristics are related to a worker's propensity to vote for the Labour Party, the question then arises which of the two is the more important in determining vote. Theoretically, as we have argued, there is no obvious reason why simply being affluent leads directly to middle-class orientations, political or otherwise. On the other hand, having been in

TABLE 28. *Voting intention by husband's earnings and by conjugal white-collar affiliations*

Husband's weekly earnings	Conjugal white-collar affiliations (family and job)	Voting intention						
		Lab.	Cons.	Lib.	Uncertain (incline to Lib. or abstain)	Abstain	Total	Nᵃ
		Percentage						
Less than £18	Both	62	33	0	0	5	100	21
	Either	81	10	5	0	5	101	42
	Neither	88	3	9	0	0	100	32
£18 or more	Both	70	15	12	3	0	100	33
	Either	70	12	10	2	6	100	49
	Neither	86	14	0	0	0	100	28

ᵃ N = 205. See note ᶜ, table 3, and note ᵃ, table 27.

close contact with middle-class persons, either through having been brought up in a white-collar family or having married into such a family, or by having worked in a white-collar job or by having a wife in such a job, are experiences which, in the light of our theoretical knowledge, *are* likely to have had a direct effect on an individual's social and political outlook. There are therefore good reasons for suspecting that the higher non-Labour vote of the more affluent workers in our sample is due not so much to their affluence as to their past or present associations with the world of the middle class. The only way in which to test this possibility is to see whether the relationship between white-collar affiliations and Labour voting persists when we control for our measures of affluence.

From table 28 we can see that the effects of white-collar affiliation on Labour voting persist when the husband's average weekly earnings are held constant. The difference between the Labour vote of the workers with high and low white-collar affiliations within the same income group is greater than the difference between the Labour vote of workers with comparable white-collar affiliations but in different income groups. The Labour vote of workers with both types of white-collar affiliation in the lower income group is much less than that of workers with neither type of affiliation in the higher income group. A striking feature of the table is that workers lacking white-collar affiliations have the highest Labour vote irrespective of income.

TABLE 29. *Voting intention by house-ownership and by conjugal white-collar affiliations*

House ownership	Conjugal white-collar affiliations (family and job)	Voting intention						
		Lab.	Cons.	Lib.	Uncertain (incline to Lib. or abstain)	Abstain	Total	N[a]
		Percentage						
Own house	Both	65	26	9	0	0	100	34
	Either	75	8	10	2	5	100	61
	Neither	83	8	8	0	0	99	24
Other	Both	70	15	5	5	5	100	20
	Either	73	17	3	0	7	100	30
	Neither	89	8	3	0	0	100	37

[a] N = 206. See note [c], table 3 and note [a], table 24.

These generalisations can be repeated exactly when house-ownership is controlled instead of income. This is shown by table 29. Workers with the strongest middle-class ties have a relatively low Labour vote irrespective of whether they are house-owners; and workers with no middle-class ties of the kind we have considered have a high Labour vote, again irrespective of ownership. It is true that within the latter group, those workers who own their own houses have a rather lower Labour vote than those who do not. But the Labour vote of those workers with the strongest middle-class ties is considerably lower than that of the house-owning workers with no such ties.

The most decisive test of the hypothesis that white-collar inter-personal influence is more important than affluence in reducing support for Labour is provided when we control for both husband's earnings and house-ownership simultaneously. As we saw in the previous chapter, this combined measure of affluence produced the greatest differentiation in Labour voting, the most affluent men (i.e. those earning £18 or more a week and owning their own house) having a considerably lower Labour vote than the least affluent men (i.e. those earning less than £18 a week and not owning a house). Table 30 sets out the voting intentions of the most and least affluent of our manual workers, each group being differentiated by degree of white-collar affiliation. It is immediately apparent that the tie between affluence and voting is to a large extent overridden. Despite their disparities in

TABLE 30. *Voting intention of most and least affluent workers by conjugal white-collar affiliations*

Husband's earnings and house-ownership	Conjugal white-collar affiliations (family and job)	Voting intention						
		Lab.	Cons.	Lib.	Uncertain (incline to Lib. or abstain)	Abstain	Total	N
		Percentage						
Men earning less than £18 and not owning own houses	Both	70	20	0	0	10	100	10
	Either	77	18	0	0	5	100	17
	Neither	91	5	5	0	0	101	23
Men earning £18 or more and owning own houses	Both	70	17	13	0	0	100	23
	Either	69	11	11	3	6	100	36
	Neither	87	13	0	0	0	100	15

earnings and ownership, the men from working-class backgrounds register a high Labour vote; and, again, despite their disparities in earnings and ownership, the workers with both types of white-collar affiliations are consistently Labour's weakest supporters.

These findings show that what we have called white-collar affiliations are clearly of much greater importance than degree of affluence in accounting for differences in voting behaviour within our sample. We are able, moreover, to confirm this point by examining the further relationship between voting and area of residence. For, in a sense, to claim that an effect on voting is exerted by the individual's area of residence may be regarded as an extension of the affluence thesis. If workers are sufficiently well off to buy their own houses, then it is likely that some of them will acquire houses in areas that are, in social terms, 'middle class'. Therefore, living in a middle-class *milieu*, they are not only more likely to be cut off from the community influences of the working-class district, but they are also more likely to be exposed to new patterns of personal influence. From the point of view of political behaviour, workers owning houses in middle-class residential areas are more likely to be surrounded by persons for whom voting Conservative is the normal thing to do. Consequently, in so far as working-class newcomers to these area are influenced by the standards

TABLE 31. *Voting intention by area of residence*

Area of residence in order of ('Residential status')	Voting intention						
	Lab.	Cons.	Lib.	Uncertain (incline to Lib. or abstain)	Abstain	Total	N^a
	Percentage						
A 'Middle class'	72	11	13	1	3	100	78
B 'Lower middle class	72	19	3	0	6	100	36
C Council estate	79	13	4	1	3	100	76
D Other private	90	10	0	0	0	100	10
E 'Slum'	100	0	0	0	0	100	7

^a N = 207. See note ^c, table 3.

of their neighbours,[1] they will be subject to cross-pressures and will react by giving fewer of their votes to Labour than workers living in areas where the population is mainly in manual, wage-earning occupations. This is a plausible hypothesis; and certainly one more meaningful than the affluence thesis couched in terms merely of income and possessions.

Information on our respondents' areas of residence was collected as part of our wider investigation. We also had at our disposal a detailed study of the ecology of Luton by Timms which conveniently classified different localities in terms of their broad social class character.[2] This classification we have taken over and used as a means of rating our respondents' areas of residence according to their 'residential status'. Table 31 sets out voting patterns by the five categories of residential areas as differentiated by Timms.[3] The majority of the men in our sample were living in either A 'middle-class' or C 'council estate' areas, the latter being preponderantly working class in social composition. As may be seen from the table, those men living in the former area registered a lower Labour vote than the council estate residents, and this is in line with the hypothesis we are considering. It would appear that area lived in has some effect on political behaviour.

[1] In this connection see, for example, Peter Willmott and Michael Young, *Family and Class in a London Suburb* (London, 1960).
[2] D. W. G. Timms, 'Distribution of Social Defectiveness in Two British Cities: A Study in Human Ecology', unpublished Ph.D. thesis, University of Cambridge (1963).
[3] Timms's classification was based on the following measures of 'residential status': distance from town centre; rateable value per house; age of housing; land use characteristics; rateable value per elector; net population density; and the 'jurors' index.

TABLE 32. *Area of residence by conjugal white-collar affiliations*

Area of residence	Both	Either	Neither	All[a]
	Conjugal white-collar affiliations (family and job)			
	Percentage			
A 'Middle class'	33	45	29	37
B 'Lower middle class'	25	19	13	18
C Council estate	30	32	50	37
D Other private	7	3	6	5
E 'Slum'	5	2	3	3
	100 (N=57)	101 (N=101)	101 (N=70)	100 (N=228)

[a] N = 228. See note [a], table 24.

TABLE 33. *Voting intention by area of residence and by conjugal white-collar affiliations*

Area of residence	Conjugal white-collar affiliations (family and job)	Lab.	Cons	Lib.	Uncertain (incline to Lib. or abstain)	Abstain	Total	N[a]
		Voting intention						
		Percentage						
A Middle class'	Both	67	17	11	0	6	101	18
	Either	70	10	15	2	2	99	40
	Neither	80	10	10	0	0	100	20
C Council estate	Both	67	20	7	7	0	101	15
	Either	72	17	3	0	7	99	29
	Neither	90	6	3	0	0	99	31

[a] N = 153. See note [a], table 24, and table 31.

However, if we now consider the alternative, 'white-collar affiliation' hypothesis, it is possible to show, first, that this factor is also related to area of residence; and secondly that, even if we hold constant area of residence, the extent of a worker's white-collar affiliations continues to be clearly associated with his voting behaviour. Table 32 demonstrates that those workers with white-collar affiliations are more often

The affluent worker: political attitudes

to be found living in 'middle-class' areas of Luton than are workers with entirely working-class backgrounds, who tend to be over-represented in the council estate area. Table 33 then shows that in both the two main types of residential area there are very marked differences in Labour voting between those workers with both family and occupational white-collar affiliations and those workers with blue-collar backgrounds. Thus the 'middle-class' attachments of our manual workers would appear to be far more important in reducing their support for Labour than their residence in 'middle-class' housing areas *per se*.

Despite the smallness of our sample, we would suggest that the systematic differences in voting that persist between workers with high and low degrees of white-collar affiliation—even when income, house-ownership, and area of residence are taken into account—are too striking to be dismissed as accidental. Furthermore, there are sound theoretical reasons why this sort of pattern should occur, and there is ample evidence in other studies to corroborate the present findings.[1]

The past and present white-collar affiliations of our manual sample clearly constitute one important variable element of their 'class situation'. The second aspect of their social affiliations which merits close attention is that of trade union membership.[2] The vast majority of our manual sample, 87% to be exact, were members of trade unions at the time of the study. Of these union members, it is true that 44% had not belonged to a union before joining their present firm. However, these men cannot all be regarded as 'green' unionists since something like two-thirds of them had been employed in their present firm for at least five years. Another 29% of the union members in the sample had been unionists prior to joining their present firm and had stayed in the same union when taking up their present employment; and a further 28% had been unionists previously but had changed to a different union on

[1] See, for example, Lipset and Bendix, *Social Mobility in Industrial Society*, pp. 64 ff.; Harold Wilensky and Hugh Edwards, 'The Skidder: Ideological Adjustments of Downward Mobile Workers', *American Sociological Review*, vol. 24 (April 1959), pp. 215–30; Richard F. Hamilton, 'The Behaviour and Values of Skilled Workers', in Arthur B. Shostak and William Gomberg (eds.), *Blue-Collar World* (New York, 1964). And in particular we would draw attention to a study of highly paid compositors in the London printing trade which found that 'social origin appears to be a more potent factor in voting behaviour than is ownership of property'. See I. C. Cannon, 'Ideology and Occupational Community', *Sociology*, vol. 1, no. 2 (May 1967), p. 169.
[2] This is discussed in detail in Goldthorpe *et al.*, *The Affluent Worker: Industrial Attitudes and Behaviour*, chapter 5.

TABLE 34. *Voting in General Election 1959 and voting intention by union membership*

Union membership	Voting in General Election 1959				Total	N[a]
	Lab.	Cons.	Lib.	Abstain		
	Percentage					
Unionists	74	13	4	10	101	182
Non-Unionists	55	28	0	17	100	29

Union membership	Voting intention					Total	N[b]
	Lab.	Cons.	Lib.	Uncertain (incline to Lib. or abstain)	Abstain		
	Percentage						
Unionists	79	12	7	1	2	101	179
Non-Unionists	61	21	7	0	11	100	28

[a] N = 211. See note [b], table 3.   [b] N = 207. See note [c], table 3.

joining their present firm. Finally, of the minority who were not union members at the time of the study, the majority, again 87%, had once been union members.

Many studies have shown that there is a definite relationship between being a trade union member and voting Labour, and our own findings confirm this generalisation. This can be seen from table 34, where it is shown that, in the General Election of 1959, three-quarters of the workers who were trade unionists voted for the Labour Party, whereas the figure for the non-unionists was just over half. A similar degree of difference in Labour support is also evident when voting intentions are considered. However, there has so far been little study of the reasons for this relationship. What are the social processes involved? There would seem to be three possible explanations.

First, it could be argued that trade union membership increases the propensity to vote Labour in that being a trade unionist brings a man under the sway of personal influences, as well as official policies, that predispose him to vote for the 'union party'.[1] The most plausible interpretation in this connection would be that, while the fact of trade union membership does not lead a man to change his party allegiance, it may, so to speak, activate him out of indifference and mobilise a potential Labour vote that would otherwise be lost through abstention. It would also seem reasonable to suggest that the longer a man's exposure to trade unionism, the more this effect of mobilisation should be apparent.

Secondly, it could be argued that men with strongly developed Labour sympathies are more likely to join trade unions and that the association between unionism and voting thus reflects in part at least a process of self-selection. This view is supported by what we know about the processes of political socialisation. Generally speaking it would appear to be the case that socialisation into political partisanship occurs at a relatively early age, usually before the individual enters the labour market and thus before he is likely to be exposed to trade unionism as a possible source of political influence. If membership of trade unions were entirely voluntary, this line of argument would suggest that there ought to be a very close association between union membership and Labour voting. But since membership is not always an entirely voluntary matter, the relationship between unionism and Labour voting will not show up so distinctly. However, the hypothesis in question does suggest that, other things being equal, the less voluntary union membership is, the less strongly it should be associated with voting Labour, and *vice versa*. This could be easily tested; but we know of no study which attempts to do so.

Finally, another explanation of the tie between unionism and Labour voting could be that both are associated to some extent with some third factor, such as, for example, the size of the plant in which workers are employed; and that this has the effect both of facilitating union organisation and of increasing working-class political consciousness.

We have set out these alternative—but not necessarily mutually exclusive—explanations, not in order to submit them to any decisive

[1] This seems to be the assumption underlying recent remarks by Perry Anderson. He holds that trade unionism is the 'one decisive phenomenon which appears to determine a worker's political allegiance far more than anything else'. He thinks that 'unionisation is the prime key to the consciousness of the British working class' because 'the union introduces the worker into a new ideological and relational universe, however minimally. It creates its own loyalty and its own logic—a logic that leads to Labour allegiance.' See 'Problems of Socialist Strategy', in Perry Anderson and Robin Blackburn (eds.), *Towards Socialism* (London, 1965), pp. 262-3.

test, but in order to clarify the issues at stake. To study the relationship between union membership and party support in a systematic way would require a longitudinal investigation and our own research was not of this kind. However, we believe that our data do enable us to say something in a tentative sort of way about the relationship involved and to raise questions for further study.

First of all, it seems unlikely that becoming a trade unionist leads a man to change his party affiliation from Conservative to Labour. Thus, although a sizable minority of our sample joined trade unions for the first time after entering their present employment, there is no evidence of any significant shift to Labour in the voting histories of this particular group of men. Moreover, as we have already noted, the currently non-union workers in the sample, who as a group are relatively strong in their support for the Conservatives, had, in the overwhelming majority of cases, once been trade unionists. Their experience of trade unionism evidently did not have the effect of pushing them in a left-wing direction; and this is confirmed by looking at their voting histories, which are consistently more right-wing than those of the sample as a whole.

This sort of finding, while it suggests that trade unionism does not have the effect of bringing about changes in voting between parties, does not of course rule out the possibility that trade unionism acts as a mobilising force for the more indifferent men who are potential Labour supporters. It has, in fact, been suggested that strength of union identification tends to increase with length of union membership;[1] and it is thus plausible that pro-Labour sentiments will also become stronger, the longer the individual has belonged to a union. Although we cannot test this hypothesis directly, one relevant finding does emerge from our data; that is, that among those men who became unionists for the first time after joining their present firm, there is a definite relationship between the length of time they had been in the firm and their propensity to vote Labour. Table 35 shows that Labour voting among this particular group of unionists steadily increases with the number of years of service in their firm, which in their case is also a rough measure of their length of exposure to unionism. And, as far as

[1] One American study had produced evidence which supports the view that 'there is a direct substantial relationship between strength of union identification and length of union membership. The longer an individual has belonged to the union, the more likely he is to identify strongly with it, and we can find no other causative factors that begin to approach this relationship in strength.' Angus Campbell, *et al.*, *The American Voter*, p. 324.

TABLE 35. *Voting intention by union status prior to joining present firm and by length of time at present firm* (*trade unionists*)

Union status	Length of Time at present firm (years)	Voting intention						
		Lab.	Cons.	Lib.	Uncertain (incline to Lib. or abstain)	Abstain	Total	N[a]
		Percentage						
Non-unionist prior to joining present firm	0–5	60	24	8	4	4	100	25
	5–15	70	20	7	0	3	100	30
	15+	82	9	9	0	0	100	22
	ALL	70	18	8	1	3	100	77
Unionist prior to joining present firm	0–5	87	6	5	0	1	99	62
	5–15	80	10	10	0	0	100	29
	15+	91	0	0	9	0	100	11
	ALL	85	7	6	1	1	100	102

[a] N = 179. See table 34.

we can tell, controlling for age does not eliminate this relationship. Thus, our data allow us to say that this category of trade unionists at any rate exhibit voting patterns which are at least consistent with the claim that an increasing exposure to trade unionism leads to a higher level of Labour support.

The other category of trade unionists—those who were union members before joining their present firm—appear to be very different. In their case, Labour voting remains remarkably high, irrespective of both age and length of service. Thus, men in this category who were under the age of 31 and who had been in their present firm for less than five years had a Labour vote of 86% as compared with a Labour vote of 91% for men who were over the age of 31 and who had been in their present firm for more than fifteen years. There would seem to be two possible explanations for this uniformly high Labour vote. First, it could be argued that length of exposure to unionism is still the vital factor, and that even the younger men with short service in their present firm might have been union members for a sufficiently long period prior to joining their firm for the influence of union membership to have had its effect. Secondly, it could be argued that men with already strongly developed Labour sympathies were more likely to have joined a trade union almost immediately on entering the labour force; that is, before taking up their present employment. Unfortunately our data do not allow us to test these alternative hypotheses.

However, no matter what the explanation for the relationship between union membership and voting may be, it is clear that whether a man is a trade unionist or not strongly affects his propensity to vote Labour. Of all the variables we consider in this study, trade union membership is only rivalled in this respect by the individual's degree of white-collar affiliation.

It is thus appropriate at this stage to examine the relative influence on voting behaviour of these two variables which we have so far dealt with separately. We may ask first of all whether those workers who have the most white-collar affiliations are least prone to be members of trade unions. As table 36 shows, there is no clear relationship of this kind in the sample taken as a whole. It is true that for our affluent workers trade union membership was not in all cases an entirely voluntary affair, and some allowance can be made for this by excluding from the analysis those workers who are employed in the firm with virtually a hundred per cent union membership—that is, Skefko. When this is done, there does appear to be a tendency for those men with both types of white-collar affiliation to be rather less likely to be trade union members than those men who have wholly blue-collar social origins and job histories.[1] However, the 'intermediate group' still stands out as the most heavily unionised of the three, and this does not therefore support the view that there is a systematic relationship between middle-class affiliations and union membership.

In the light of these findings, it is then of some interest to ask next whether white-collar affiliations continue to exert an influence on voting when union membership is held constant. From table 37 we can see that in the General Election of 1959 the expected relationship between this variable and Labour support is clearly present. There is a difference of seventeen percentage points between the Labour vote of unionists with both types of white-collar affiliation and that of unionists with entirely blue-collar affiliations. It may also be noted that, among those workers in the latter category, union membership seems to make no difference whatsoever to the level of Labour voting. This is particularly interesting because it will be remembered that the high Labour vote of

[1] This was also the finding of S. M. Lipset and Joan Gordon in their study of labour mobility in Oakland, California, in 1949. See 'Mobility and Trade Union Membership' in R. Bendix and S. M. Lipset (eds.), *Class, Status and Power* (Glencoe, 1953), p. 493.

TABLE 36. *Trade union membership by conjugal white-collar affiliations*

Union membership	Conjugal white-collar affiliations (family and job)		
	Both	Either	Neither
	Percentage		
Entire sample			
Unionist	79	93	84
Non-unionist	21	7	16
	100 (N = 57)	100 (N = 101)	100 (N = 70)
Excluding men employed at Skefko			
Unionist	63	85	73
Non-unionist	37	15	27
	100 (N = 30)	100 (N = 48)	100 (N = 41)

men with no white-collar affiliations was similarly unaffected by variations in the level of husband's earnings and house ownership (table 22 above). It would seem, therefore, that men from such 'solid working-class' backgrounds are likely to be heavily pro-Labour irrespective of whether they are well off or not, in a union or outside it.

When we turn to voting intentions (table 38) the white-collar affiliation effect is still present, although within the trade unionist group it discriminates less strongly than it does in the previous table. We cannot unequivocally say that the reduced effect of the variable does not represent a genuine leftward shift among those workers with the more middle-class backgrounds. But on the whole, we would regard the data on reported voting in the election of 1959 as a more reliable description of party attachment than that on voting intentions.[1] And moreover, quite apart from this consideration, there is another factor operating which tends to *reduce* the effect of the white-collar affiliation variable in both tables: namely, union status prior to joining the firm.

We already know that those men who were trade unionists before joining their present firms have a higher Labour vote than those who first became unionists after joining their present firm. As may be seen from

---

[1] The proportion of actual abstentions will be higher than the proportion of intended abstentions; and some of the men who were uncertain (the don't knows) will actually vote for a party. If the latter are allocated on the basis of their party choice in 1959, the trade unionists with both family and job white-collar affiliations have an intended Labour vote of 73% as opposed to an intended Labour vote of 83% among trade unionists with purely blue-collar affiliations.

TABLE 37. *Voting at General Election 1959 by trade union membership and by conjugal white-collar affiliations*

Union status	Conjugal white-collar affiliations (family and job)	Voting in General Election in 1959				Total	Nᵃ
		Lab.	Cons.	Lib.	Abstain		
		Percentage					
Trade unionists	Both	64	19	7	10	100	42
	Either	73	12	5	10	100	86
	Neither	81	9	0	9	99	53
Non-unionists	Both	42	42	0	16	100	12
	Either	43	28	0	28	99	7
	Neither	80	10	0	10	100	10

ᵃ N = 210. See note ᵇ, table 3, and note ᵃ, table 24.

TABLE 38. *Voting intention by trade union membership and by conjugal white-collar affiliations*

Union status	Conjugal white-collar affiliations (family and job)	Voting intention					Total	Nᵃ
		Lab.	Cons.	Lib.	Uncertain (incline to Lib. or abstain)	Abstain		
		Percentage						
Trade unionists	Both	76	17	5	2	0	100	42
	Either	76	11	8	1	4	100	85
	Neither	84	10	6	0	0	100	51
Non-unionists	Both	33	42	17	0	8	100	12
	Either	50	17	0	0	33	100	6
	Neither	100	0	0	0	0	100	10

ᵃ N = 206. See note ᶜ, table 3, and note ᵃ, table 24.

table 35, this difference is quite substantial, the intended Labour vote of the former group being 70% and that of the latter 85%. It could be, therefore, that the association between white-collar affiliation and Labour voting within the trade unionist group is due to the fact that among the unionists with extensive white-collar affiliations, there is a higher proportion of men who were non-unionists prior to joining their present firm than there is among the unionists with wholly blue-

TABLE 39. *Voting in General Election 1959 and voting intention by union status prior to joining present firm and by conjugal white-collar affiliations (trade unionists)*

Union status prior to joining present firm	Conjugal white-collar affiliations (family and job)	Voting in General Election 1959					
		Lab.	Cons.	Lib.	Abstain	Total	N[a]
		Percentage					
Non-unionist previously	Both	58	33	8	0	99	12
	Either	58	21	7	14	100	43
	Neither	80	12	0	8	100	25
Unionist previously	Both	67	13	7	13	100	30
	Either	88	2	2	7	99	43
	Neither	82	7	0	11	100	28

		Voting intention					
		Lab.	Cons.	Lib.	Uncertain (incline to Lib. or abstain)	Abstain	Total	N[a]
		Percentage					
Non-unionist previously	Both	64	27	9	0	0	100	11
	Either	68	17	7	2	5	99	41
	Neither	76	16	8	0	0	100	25
Unionist previously	Both	81	13	3	3	0	100	31
	Either	84	5	9	0	2	100	44
	Neither	92	4	4	0	0	100	26

[a] N = 181. See table 27. [b] N = 178. See table 38.

collar affiliations. However, as table 39 shows, quite the reverse is true. Over 70% of the men with both family and occupational white-collar affiliations were trade union members *before* joining their present firm; whereas in the other two groups, the figure is approximately 50%. We have no data which can provide a conclusive explanation of why this particular group of men should be more likely to have been unionists prior to joining their present firm than the men whose family and occupational affiliations are wholly blue collar. But the fact that they are 'accidentally' over-represented in this way means that the level of Labour voting among trade unionists who have both types of white-collar affiliation (as set out in tables 37 and 38 above) would be correspondingly lower, were their distribution by union status prior to joining their present firm brought into line with that of the other trade unionists.

But even if allowance were made for this factor, the trade unionists with white-collar backgrounds would still continue to give a noticeably higher proportion of their votes to the Labour Party than would men of similar backgrounds who are not members of trade unions. And, as table 39 shows, a similar generalisation holds true with respect to union status prior to joining the firm. Thus, in the General Election of 1959, men with both family and occupational white-collar affiliations were more likely to support Labour if they had been in a trade union before they joined their present firm than if they had become union members subsequently. A similar pattern is also evident in the voting intentions of these same men in 1964. In the case of workers with extensive 'middle-class' affiliations, then, trade union membership and also, probably, length of union membership do seem to be related to the propensity to vote for the Labour Party.

However, when we turn to the workers with no white-collar affiliations, we see that both categories of trade union members showed an equally strong preference for Labour in the election of 1959. This provides further confirmation of the previously noted tendency for workers from wholly blue-collar backgrounds to be relatively 'solid' Labour supporters, irrespective of level of affluence, and of trade union membership. The data on voting intentions yield a somewhat different, though not entirely inconsistent finding. The men who had been trade unionists before joining their present firm were intending to support Labour much more heavily than were the men who had not become unionists until they joined their present firm. Yet this difference, which is certainly substantial, would appear to be due more to the exceptionally high proportion of intending Labour voters in the former group than to an unusually low proportion of such voters in the latter group.

Given the small sample of workers we are dealing with, our conclusions regarding the relative influence on voting of trade union membership and white-collar affiliations can be no more than tentative. Nevertheless, it does seem that on the whole those workers with neither family nor occupational affiliations of a white-collar kind are the men whose high level of support for Labour is least affected by such factors

71

as earnings, house-ownership, and trade union membership. In all the breakdowns that we have made in this chapter, there is only one instance in which the proportion of Labour supporters among any section of this particular group has been less than 80%.[1] On the other hand, among the workers with the most extensive white-collar affiliations, trade union membership would seem to have a more noticeable effect in increasing Labour voting. This tendency for trade union membership to differ in its effects on the voting behaviour of these two groups is understandable in terms of the networks of social relations in which they are involved and of the personal influences which bear upon them. Thus manual workers with no white-collar affiliations may be regarded as the least 'cross-pressured' group in our sample; and it would appear that in their case the mutually reinforcing effects of their 'working-class' jobs and their 'working-class' social backgrounds produce such a relatively high level of Labour voting that union membership can have little additional influence. By contrast, the men with the extensive white-collar affiliations should be the most 'cross-pressured' group, being pulled in one direction by the nature of their 'working-class' occupations and in the opposite direction by their past and present associations with 'middle-class' individuals. If this is so, then it might be argued that in their case trade union membership, through exposing them to another source of 'working-class' influence, would make relatively more difference to their propensity to vote Labour than it would among workers from wholly blue-collar backgrounds.[2]

[1] And in this instance it was 76% (table 39).
[2] We are conscious that, throughout the above analysis, we have based our discussion almost entirely on differences between these two groups of workers. However, in view of the fact that we found it necessary to use a rather crude measure of 'white-collar affiliation', we feel that limiting our comparisons to these two extreme groups is a legitimate procedure.

5. Conclusion

The major finding of this study is that, in so far as their political behaviour is concerned, no process of *embourgeoisement* is evident among our sample of affluent manual workers. The sample we chose was one in which the political consequences of the 'worker turning middle class' should have been very pronounced. Our men were not only 'middle class' in terms of their incomes and possessions, but they were working in industries and living in communities which were in various respects markedly different from those of the more traditional working class. Yet we have found no evidence of any shift in their political loyalties away from the Labour Party. On the contrary, their voting histories show that they have been and continue to be notably staunch Labour supporters.

This finding did not, however, surprise us. Before beginning our research, we had argued—on the basis of theoretical considerations— that the radical changes in attitudes and behaviour implied by the concept of *embourgeoisement* were unlikely to be occurring on a large scale in British society; and certainly not as a result of increasing prosperity alone. The simple argument that working-class affluence leads to a 'middle-class' style of life, and that this in turn leads to a decrease in Labour voting, takes no account of the social structure in which class attitudes are formed and maintained. Indeed, the facts on which the affluence thesis has been based have in the main been gathered by means of poll-type social surveys, and it is a weakness of such investigations that they tend to concentrate on individual charac- teristics—such as age, sex, level of income and education—and fail to take into account the properties of the social structures in which the individuals in question are located; for example, those of work organ- isations and local communities. In approaching the problem of the 'affluent worker' we assumed that these structural factors were of basic importance to an understanding of changes in working-class life, and our research was designed in such terms.[1] As we noted in the intro- ductory chapter, our aim was to study a sample of workers whose

[1] See Lockwood and Goldthorpe, 'The Manual Worker: Affluence, Aspirations and Assimilation'; and Goldthorpe and Lockwood, 'Affluence and the British Class Structure'.

industrial and community *milieux* were lacking the distinctive features of traditional working-class life. In this concluding chapter, therefore, a brief characterisation of the social bases of political attitudes and behaviour in the traditional working class may usefully serve to provide a perspective on what we have found out about the 'new' and affluent working class.

As we use it, the 'traditional worker' is a sociological rather than a historical concept; in other words, it refers more to workers in particular industrial and community settings than to the working class as a whole at some particular point of time. Thus, by no means all of the pre-war working class were traditional in our sense, and in the post-war period distinctive elements of working-class traditionalism still persist in various parts of the country. Moreover, the concept of the traditional worker encompasses not only the most class-conscious and most radical sections of the working class (what we shall call 'proletarian traditionalists') but also its socially most conservative elements ('deferential traditionalists').[1] The following discussion will be confined to the former group, who, relative to other sections of the working class, are particularly solid Labour supporters.

The most highly developed forms of proletarian traditionalism seem to be particularly closely associated with industries such as mining, docking, fishing and shipbuilding; that is, with industries which tend to concentrate workers together in solidary communities and to isolate them from the influences of the wider society. Normally, most of the workers in such occupations have a high degree of job involvement, and close attachments to primary work groups that possess a relatively high degree of autonomy from technical and supervisory constraints. Pride in doing 'men's work' and an awareness of shared occupational experiences make for a strongly developed industrial *camaraderie* which is frequently expressed through a distinctive work culture. Thus primary groups of workmates not only provide the elementary units of more extensive class loyalties, but work associations also carry over into leisure activities, so that workers in these industries usually participate in what are called occupational communities. That is to say, workmates are preferred leisure-time companions, often also neighbours, and not infrequently kinsmen. The existence of such closely knit cliques of friends, workmates, neighbours and relatives is indeed

---

[1] See David Lockwood, 'Sources of Variation in Working Class Images of Society', *Sociological Review*, vol. 14, no. 3 (November 1966).

the hallmark of the traditional working-class community.[1] The values expressed through these social networks emphasise mutual aid in everyday life and the obligation to join in the gregarious pattern of leisure, which itself demands the expenditure of time, money and energy in a public- and present-oriented conviviality and inhibits individual striving 'to be different'. As a form of social life, this communal sociability has a ritualistic quality, creating a high 'moral density' and reinforcing sentiments of belonging to a work-dominated collectivity. The socially isolated and endogamous nature of the community, its predominantly one-class population, and low rates of geographical and social mobility all tend to make for an inward-looking society and to accentuate the sense of class identity that springs from shared work experiences.

In this type of setting, loyalty to the Labour Party is but one expression of a more general social outlook which we have termed 'solidaristic collectivism'.[2] We use this phrase to indicate a disposition towards collective forms of action which is based on a consciousness of belonging to a working-class community. Thus in this situation political allegiance is more or less ascribed to the individual by virtue of his membership of the community. For such traditional workers the Labour Party is, in Duverger's words, *the* 'community party'.[3] Because of the nature of the social structure in which he lives, the worker is seldom exposed to influences that might alter his political convictions; on the contrary, everything in his social environment, at work and at leisure, combines to render them beyond question. Party allegiance is less a conscious and deliberate choice than a by-product of the more primitive forms of collectivism in which he is involved at the workplace, in the local union branch, in the working-men's club, and, at an even deeper level, in the communal sociability of everyday life. These forms of social relationship make his support for Labour the 'natural' or 'instinctive' one; the political reflection of a class consciousness which makes a sharp division between the world of 'us', the ordinary working-men, and that of 'them', the bosses and those in authority generally.

[1] The one-industry town with its dominant occupational community would seem to produce the most distinctive forms of proletarian traditionalism. But, given a relatively isolated community with a stable and preponderantly working-class population, a quite high degree of proletarian traditionalism is perfectly compatible with industrial diversification. See, for example, Richard Hoggart, *The Uses of Literacy* (London, 1959); and Michael Young and Peter Willmott, *Family and Kinship in East London* (London, 1959).

[2] See Goldthorpe and Lockwood, 'Affluence and the British Class Structure'.

[3] Maurice Duverger, *Political Parties* (London, 1962), pp. 116, 124–32.

6-2

The affluent worker: political attitudes

This picture of the traditional worker is, of course, overdrawn. But nevertheless it provides a useful benchmark against which to set the salient characteristics of the new working class, since the change from the old to the new is best understood in terms of changes which have come about in the traditional structure. In this respect, greater prosperity and growing ownership of houses and consumer durables among manual workers have been less important than changes in their distribution by industry, occupation and locality. In particular, the industries and occupations in which the traditional worker is most typically to be found are declining relatively to more modern, especially mass-production, industries. The one-industry town is less and less a familiar aspect of British industrial society, and so too are the working-class 'districts' in the centres of large towns and cities. Concomitantly with industrial and occupational diversification there has occurred the breakup of these more traditional working-class communities through the voluntary and involuntary residential mobility of their populations. Such a process has been going on for several decades, but it is in the post-war years that it has become more and more evident as a major source of change in working-class attitudes and behaviour.

In terms of social values, the transition from the traditional to the new working class may be seen as a change from 'solidaristic collectivism' towards what we would term a more 'instrumental' orientation—to work, trade unionism and politics alike. And, in terms of social relationships, a parallel movement may be suggested: away from 'communal sociability' towards a more 'privatised' form of social existence, in which the economic advancement of the individual and his family becomes of greater importance than membership in a closely knit local community. These at any rate, were the guiding lines of our research. If there was any truth in the assertion that working-class prosperity was leading to a diffusion of middle-class attitudes and styles of life, then it seemed to us that this process would be most in evidence among workers who were outside the sway of the traditional ethos. And, as we have explained in chapter I, the workers we studied were selected to meet this requirement.[1] However, this does not mean

---

[1] In this we were successful, and the data we have collected more than justify the usefulness of the distinctions referred to above. The companion monograph on the industrial attitudes and behaviour of affluent workers, and work in preparation on their patterns of community life, take these themes of 'instrumentalism', 'privatisation' and 'status segregation' as their major organising principles. An outline of our findings is presented in Goldthorpe *et al.*, 'The Affluent Worker and the Thesis of *Embourgeoisement*'.

that we accepted the view that, even under such conditions, *embourgeoisement* would be the necessary consequence of working-class affluence. And certainly so far as political attitudes and behaviour are concerned, we could see no compelling reason why the new and affluent working class should not be strong Labour supporters, even though the motives for this support might be different from those of the traditional worker.

This conclusion stemmed from our reading of previous studies of the style of life and central life interests of the new working class. Taken in combination with what is known about the market situation of the industrial worker, these data suggested that the pursuit of private economic betterment by the new working class might even strengthen their commitment to forms of collective action which can further the attainment of their goals as individuals. First of all, it is reasonable to suppose that the workplace and the local community are of less and less significance as sources of social integration among the type of workers in whom we are interested; and that, in consequence, the economic advancement of the 'privatised' nuclear family is becoming the major concern of the industrial worker. If this is so, then it is clear that, so far as the majority of such workers are concerned, the means for realising this goal are limited to either an individual search for more remunerative work or trade union action to improve wages and conditions of service in their present employment.[1] Even then, these are not really alternative possibilities on a large scale because although a worker may move to a different firm in search of higher earnings, once he is there he is powerless as a single individual to maintain or to improve his economic status. In the great majority of cases, workers do not of course regard job mobility and trade union membership as alternatives, but rather as supplementary to one another; especially in large firms, where most of the affluent working class are to be found. Therefore, in spite of increasing prosperity and the attenuation of more traditional forms of class consciousness, the new industrial worker is still in a position where collective action is the chief means by which he can maintain and improve his economic position. Moreover, as we have already noted, there are grounds for believing that by comparison with the traditional worker this desire for higher wages is particularly central in

[1] Of other possible means, upward mobility into the higher echelons of white-collar work is less and less of a possibility; and 'setting up on one's own', while a 'dream' that was mentioned by many of the men in our sample, is a realistic way out of manual wage-earning for only a tiny minority.

77

the motivation of the new working class. In the first place, the increased importance of a family-centred style of life—with all that this implies for the value set on a progressively increasing standard of living, especially in the form of consumer durables—is likely to make wages a *more* crucial issue than among the traditional working class, who, as one aspect of their traditionalism, tend to have more fixed and stable levels of aspiration. And, secondly, the kinds of semi-skilled jobs through which the great majority of industrial workers obtain their affluence are also jobs which offer few other rewards and satisfactions; thus a central feature of the 'instrumental' orientation to work that seems characteristic of workers in such jobs is an unusual degree of 'money-mindedness'.

Given that there are compelling reasons why affluent workers should use collective means to obtain their private ends, this does not, of course, imply that they will automatically be supporters of the Labour Party—although we can say, at the very least, that there is nothing incompatible between the two. Nevertheless, it is quite conceivable that a worker might feel that his personal economic interest could best be served by joining a trade union *and* by voting for the Conservative or the Liberal Party. But again, as a matter of fact, we know from a number of studies that workers are much more likely to vote for the Labour Party if they are trade union members; and since we have already argued that there are good reasons for believing that the majority of new and affluent workers will be strongly inclined to join trade unions, then we can assume that the practice, if not the logic, of privatised self-interest will normally result in a relatively high Labour vote among the new and affluent working class.

While the nature of the relationship between trade union member-ship and voting for the Labour Party is in need of further study, it is not difficult to understand how both have a common basis in the work situation of the industrial employee. For, despite his affluence, the worker's experience of the social divisions of the work-place, of the power and remoteness of management, and of his own inconsiderable chances of ever being anything but a manual wage-earner all generally dispose him to think of himself as a member of the class of 'ordinary workers', and to seek collective rather than individualistic solutions to his problems. Although the 'new' worker's class consciousness may be much weaker than that of the traditional worker and may not extend much beyond his own particular work-place, it is probably still the most powerful single influence affecting his sense of social identity. And this is perhaps all the more likely to be so since members of the new working class tend to live a relatively privatised social life outside of work. For while they are no longer involved in working-class communities of the traditional type, they do not appear to have become integrated to any great extent into middle-class society either. In our own study, for example, we found that while our affluent workers enjoyed a standard of living comparable to that of many white-collar families, their social worlds were still, in the great majority of cases, separate from those of the latter. Nor was there much indication that affluence had encouraged a desire on the part of these workers to *seek* acceptance in new social *milieux* at higher status levels.[1] Thus, although the division between 'us' and 'them' may have become less evident in terms of income and living standards, and at the same time less dominant in the workers' 'image' of the social order, it is nonetheless one which still in fact persists in the relationships of both work and community life.

On the basis of these considerations, then, it did not surprise us to find that a high proportion of the men in our sample proved to be regular Labour voters. At the same time, the analysis we have presented led us to expect that, by contrast with more traditional workers, the new working class would have a much more pronounced 'instrumental' attitude to trade unionism and to party politics; and that the quality, if not the degree, of adherence to the Labour Party would be different. As far as our workers' attitudes to their employment and trade union membership are concerned, this thesis would appear to have much validity.[2] As regards their political attitudes, the evidence is less clear-cut. It would, of course, be out of line with the findings of a great deal of research in electoral sociology to suppose that a majority of people can take a *purely* instrumental view of their political allegiances, if by this is meant that the individual makes a precise calculation of all the specific advantages and disadvantages that are likely to affect him personally as a result of the victory of one party or another. This extreme form of instrumentalism is not what we had in mind. We expected rather that, in giving reasons for supporting the Labour Party, the new working class would give greater prominence to the social and economic benefits of a Labour Government and would

[1] See Goldthorpe *et al.*, 'The Affluent Worker and the Thesis of *Embourgeoisement*', pp. 20–3.
[2] See Goldthorpe *et al.*, '*The Affluent Worker: Industrial Attitudes and Behaviour*', chapters 2 and 5 especially.

be correspondingly less moved by sentiments of class loyalty. In fact, as we have seen, the conception of the Labour Party as a 'class party'— as a party appropriate to the 'ordinary working man'—is one that still figures largely in the political consciousness of the workers in our sample. In this respect our workers do not seem to differ very markedly from working-class supporters of Labour in general. But instrumental attitudes having to do with the 'pay-off' to be expected from a Labour Government in the way of higher living standards and better social services were also clearly in evidence. Indeed, such considerations were dominant in the replies given by the Labour supporters in our sample when they were evaluating the significance of a Labour victory at the next General Election. Of course, since most of them had become affluent during a long period of Conservative rule, it could be that such attitudes were less an expression of instrumentalism based on past experience than an expression of hopes based on a more diffuse sense of attachment to Labour. None the less, other data we collected did suggest that our workers' overwhelming support for Labour was of a less 'solidaristic' nature than that of the traditional working class. Here we are referring to the findings that only a bare majority of the men who were both trade union members and intending Labour voters were in favour of the existing link between the trade union movement and the Labour Party and that a quarter of the same group had deliberately 'contracted out' of paying the political levy to their trade union. There is thus definitely some evidence in support of the idea of instrumental collectivism as far as the political orientations of our men are concerned—although perhaps less than our analysis had led us to expect.

One further question which is prompted at this point is that of whether a decline in 'solidaristic' relative to more 'instrumental' political orientations in the new working class need necessarily result in a lower and less stable level of support for the Labour Party. As far as our own study is concerned, we have found no indication that the Labour vote of our men is lacking stability; and, chiefly because of the general features of their employment as manual wage-earners, we see little reason why their level of Labour voting should not remain stable, even though it may be determined by relatively instrumental considerations. On the other hand, the actual level of Labour voting in our sample *is* probably somewhat lower than it is among the workers we have called proletarian traditionalists. But to the extent that it is lower, we would attribute this less to differences in the character of the two types of collectivism that we have been discussing than to the fact that, within the new working class, there are proportionately more men for whom collectivism as such has relatively less appeal because of their social origins and job histories. This last point seems in fact to be of major relevance to the whole question of working-class *embourgeoisement*.

We have seen that those men in our sample who had particularly extensive white-collar affiliations were markedly less likely to vote for the Labour Party than men whose family and occupational background were entirely blue collar. Moreover, even when the former group did support the Labour Party, they were less likely to visualise it as a 'class party' and to view as desirable the existing relationship between the trade union movement and the Labour Party. It was also the case that the workers with extensive white-collar affiliations were more likely to have instrumental attitudes towards their employment, and to have patterns of social life which were closer to those of the middle class.[1] These tendencies, though of course requiring further examination than was possible with our relatively small sample, strengthen our belief that it is the extent of workers' family or occupational 'bridges' with the middle class, rather than such factors as level of earnings or standards of consumption, which provides the key to possible changes within the working class in the direction of *embourgeoisement*.[2] No more than a minority of manual workers can have extensive ties with the middle class; but, we would think, it is highly probable that this is a growing minority in the country at large. Most importantly in this respect, the long-run trends for white-collar employment to expand more rapidly than blue-collar work and for women to take up an increasing proportion of white-collar jobs must mean that more manual wage-earners will have siblings and wives who are 'middle class' in terms at least of occupational status. Consequently, then, if the fore-going analysis has any validity, it is precisely such changes in the occupational structure, rather than affluence itself, that must be regarded as possibly the most influential factor in encouraging the spread of middle-class values and life-styles among the working class.[3]

[1] On the first point, see Goldthorpe *et al.*, *The Affluent Worker: Industrial Attitudes and Behaviour*, chapter 7; the second statement is based on findings that will be presented in subsequent publications.

[2] See David Lockwood, 'The "New Working Class"', p. 256.

[3] Evidence from studies of educational achievement indicates the importance of such family bridges for status aspiration in the working class. The latest and most detailed

The affluent worker: political attitudes

On the political level, this could of course mean a decline in support for the Labour Party with underlying causes that are more systematic, if less widespread in their effect, than those which have been held to be associated with working-class prosperity. However, before any such hypothesis may be seriously considered, there is need for much detailed study of the relative importance for political behaviour of both the number and different forms of white-collar affiliations. At the same time, the effects of such affiliations must be weighed against the social pressures of the work-place and trade unionism which, in general, provide a political education that runs counter to any middle-class influence which workers may experience by virtue of their social origins and previous occupational connections. In this study we have been able to do little more than indicate the significance of these variables and much remains to be done in the way of exploring their interrelations. But as to their importance there can be no doubt: the understanding of contemporary working-class politics is to be found, first and foremost, in the structure of the worker's group attachments and not, as many have suggested, in the extent of his income and possessions.

investigation is that of Douglas, *The Home and the School*. By far the most illuminating analysis of *embourgeoisement* from the point of view of family role structure is to be found in the work of Basil Bernstein. See particularly 'A Socio-linguistic Approach to Socialisation: with reference to educability', in D. Hymes and J. Gumperz (eds.), *The Ethnology of Communication* (New York, 1968).

Appendix A. Response rates by firms and type of work

TABLE A 1. *Response rates by firm and type of work*

Firm and type of work	Number in original sample	Number interviewed (work)	Response percentage	Number interviewed (home)	Overall response percentage
Vauxhall assembly	127	100	79	86	68
Skefko					
machining	65	45	69	41	63
machine setting	31	23	74	23	74
maintenance etc.	58	46	79	45	78
All Skefko	154	114	74	109	71
Laporte					
process work	31	23	74	23	74
maintenance	14	13	93	11	79
All Laporte	45	36	80	34	76
TOTALS	326	250	77	229	70

Appendix B. A note on the sample

The 'population' of the critical case with which our study was concerned is described on p. 4 of the text. Our interviewing sample is not a random one of this population. In regard to each of the occupational categories in question—assemblers at Vauxhall, machinists, craftsmen and setters at Skefko, and process workers and craftsmen at Laporte—the sample is based on men in these categories who worked in certain selected departments. In Vauxhall, our assemblers were drawn from six of the major assembly divisions in the plant: the four- and six-cylinder engine assembly lines, the body and trim shops on the car line, and the body and trim shops on the van or 'commercial' line. In Skefko, our machine operators and setters came from a number of the largest machine shops covering heavy grinding, turret-lathe turning and 'automatic' turning; and the craftsmen were taken from the plant's two millwrights' shops and from the toolroom. In Laporte, the process workers and maintenance craftsmen came from all process departments which were in full production—that is, which were not engaged on pilot schemes.

The difficulty of such a sample is obvious: one cannot generalise from it to the population except on the assumption that the respondents from the departments which were taken were in each case representative of all the men in the occupational category concerned. However, while this was recognised, the course which was actually pursued commended itself for the following reasons: (i) in some cases the administrative problems which would have been involved in covering all relevant departments would have exceeded management's willingness to co-operate; (ii) for each department included, some appreciable time had to be spent with the managers, supervisors and union officials concerned explaining, and securing agreement to, our interviewing procedures; (iii) in each department, too, a still greater amount of time was required to discover 'how things worked', so that intelligent interviewing could be carried out, and to make an adequate observational survey; (iv) with every occupational category it appeared—and proved—possible to take in most of the larger departments in which men who met our specifications on age, marital status, earnings and residence appeared to be concentrated, with the result that within each category an estimated 60–70% of our population was in fact covered. On this basis, then, and since we could find no grounds for supposing that the men left out differed widely from those included, we would feel that the assumption may reasonably be made that in this respect our sample will not, at least, be seriously misleading.

Within the departments we selected, our aim was then—in principle—

to invite for interview *all* those men who came within our population. This was desirable in most cases in order to secure a sufficiently large number of respondents to permit useful statistical analysis of our interview material. This policy proved feasible, and was in fact implemented, in all the departments in question with the exception of the two largest of the Vauxhall assembly divisions—the body and trim shops on the car line. Here, the number involved made further sampling necessary and this was carried out on a random basis from personnel records. This complication meant, of course, both that the assemblers in the two departments in question were under-represented within their occupational category and that the assemblers generally were under-represented in our sample. To correct for these imbalances, some form of appropriate 'weighting' could, and strictly speaking should, have been introduced. However, in the first respect, there proved to be little point in doing this since a careful check on the interview material revealed no systematic differences in the pattern of response of the men from the car-line divisions and that of the rest of the assemblers. Thus, weighted results would not in the main have differed sufficiently to affect the interpretation of the data from the percentage figures produced by taking all the assemblers together on an equal basis. In the second respect, the under-representation of the assemblers generally could, of course, seriously affect our conclusions regarding the pattern of response of the sample as a whole (as in chapter 2 above) if the voting behaviour of the assemblers were markedly different from that of our other affluent workers. In fact, as may be seen from table B 1, the proportion of assemblers who were intending to vote Labour at the time of the interviews was only slightly lower than the corresponding figure for the sample as a whole—72% as opposed to 76%. Considering the Labour vote as a proportion of votes intended for the three main parties, 77% of the assemblers supported Labour as opposed to a figure of 79% for the entire sample. It is true that by comparison with the other occupational groups in our sample the assemblers are the least in favour of the Labour Party.[1] At the same time, by comparison with manual workers in general, the proportion of Labour voters among the assemblers is still relatively high. Thus, even if allowance were made for the fact that the assemblers are under-represented in our sample, the results would differ only marginally from the findings we have presented in this monograph, and our main line of argument would remain unchanged.

[1] A more detailed occupational breakdown shows that the workers least likely to vote Labour are a sub-group of the Skefko setters (those working on 'automatics'), 15 men in all. The position of the setters generally is discussed in Goldthorpe *et al.*, *The Affluent Worker: Industrial Attitudes and Behaviour*, where it is noted that these workers, whose work attitudes and behaviour are in many respects distinctive, are also men who have experienced some limited but real degree of job mobility.

Appendix B

TABLE B I. *Voting intention by occupational group*

Occupational group	Voting intention						
	Lab.	Cons.	Lib.	Uncertain (incline to Lib. or abstain)	Abstain	Total	N
	Percentage						
Vauxhall assemblers	72	15	6	1	5	99	79
Skefko machinists and setters	77	18	4	0	2	101	56
Laporte process	76	10	10	0	5	101	21
Laporte and Skefko craftsmen	82	6	10	2	0	100	51
ALL	76	13	7	1	3	100	207[a]

[a] N = 207. See note [c], table 3.

Appendix C. A note on the classification of 'voting history' and 'attachment' to party

Sections (*a*) and (*b*) of table C 1 give details of the classification of the 'voting histories' of our respondents. This is based on their reports of how they voted, if eligible, in each General Election from 1945 to 1959, inclusive. Section (*c*) of the same table explains how these 'voting histories' were used, in combination with our respondents' voting intentions at the time of the investigation, to classify their 'party attachments'.

It may be noted that of the 26 men whose 'voting history' was classified as 'uncommitted', the majority was made up of those who had abstained from voting either on the first occasion on which they were eligible to vote (13 men), *or* on the first *and* second occasions after they become eligible (4 men); that is, the majority were young abstainers.

There were 9 men in all who had actually switched from voting Labour to voting Conservative, and *vice versa*. Of the 3 men whose first vote was Conservative, 1 became a Labour voter in 1950, and the other 2 in 1959. Of the 6 men whose first vote was Labour, 4 switched to Conservative in 1950 (1 of these men changed back to voting Labour in 1959), 1 in 1951, and 1 in 1959.

TABLE C 1

(*a*) *Distribution of respondents by 'voting history' 1945–1959*

Voting history	No.	Percentage
'Solid' Labour	131	62
'Solid' Conservative	18	9
'Solid' Liberal	—	—
'Irregular' Labour	12	6
'Irregular' Conservative	6	3
'Irregular' Liberal	1	1
'Deviationist' Labour	3	1
'Deviationist' Conservative	1	1
'Deviationist' Liberal	—	—
'Uncommitted'	26	12
'Changers'	13	6
	211	101

Appendix C

(b) *Definitions used in classifying 'voting history'*

'Solid' = Have always voted whenever eligible and always for the same party.

'Irregular' = Have always voted for the same party but may have abstained as often as voted (but not more often).

'Deviationist' = Must have been eligible to vote on three or more occasions. Conservative or Labour 'deviationists' may have 'deviated' by voting Liberal once in *three* eligibilities, or may have 'deviated to Liberal once and abstained once in *four* eligibilities. Liberal 'deviationists' are defined in the same way except that they have 'deviated' to *either* Labour *or* Conservative.

'Uncommitted' = Have abstained on every occasion on which they were eligible to vote, or have abstained more often than they have voted, and have never voted for both Conservative and Labour.

'Changer' = All those who have ever voted for Conservative *and* Labour (9 men), plus those whose 'deviations' to Liberal voting from Conservative or Labour voting were too frequent for them to be classified as 'deviationists' (4).

(c) *Classification of party 'attachment'*

This was based on 'voting history' 1945–59 and voting intention 1963–4. All men whose 'voting history' was classified as 'solid' or 'irregular' Labour or Conservative were regarded as being 'attached' to their party provided that they were not intending to change their party allegiance. In the case of Labour and Conservative 'deviationists', these were also classified as being 'attached' to their party except where their voting intention showed that their 'deviation' was continuing (e.g. an intended vote of Liberal after a 'voting history' of Labour, Labour, Liberal, or Conservative, Liberal, Conservative).

88

Appendix D. The occupational classification used in the study

The occupational classification set out in the first column of table D 1 below was constructed on the basis of previous efforts by British sociologists, notably that of Hall and Caradog Jones.[1] The particular occupational classification used in this and other reports on the research has been derived from this more comprehensive eight-fold classification through collapsing categories in whatever ways appeared most useful from case to case. The threefold classification into 'white-collar', 'intermediate', and 'manual' occupations that is used in the present monograph is given in the last column of table D 1.

In allocating particular occupations to classes of occupations we followed the general rule of choosing the 'lower' alternative in all bordering cases or cases where our information was incomplete or ambiguous. The examples given below are selected in order to give some idea of the range of occupations included in given categories as well as of 'typical' occupations.

Table D 2 shows the relationship between voting intention, age, and degree of white-collar affiliation.

[1] J. Hall and D. Caradog Jones, 'The Social Grading of Occupations,' *British Journal of Sociology*, vol. I, (January 1950).

Appendix D

TABLE D I. *Occupational classification*

Occupational status level	Examples	Summary classification used as basis for 'white-collar affiliation' groupings
1 (a) Higher professional, managerial and other white-collar employees	Chartered accountant, business executive, senior civil servant, graduate teacher	
(b) Large industrial or commercial employers, landed proprietors	—	
2 (a) Intermediate professional, managerial and other white-collar employees	Pharmacist, non-graduate teacher, departmental manager, bank cashier	
(b) Medium industrial or commercial employers, substantial farmers	—	'White collar'
3 (a) Lower professional, managerial and other white-collar employees	Chiropodist, bar manager, commercial traveller, draughtsman, accounts or wages clerk	
(b) Small industrial or commercial employers, small proprietors, small farmers	Jobbing builder, taxi owner-driver, tobacconist	
4 (a) Supervisory, inspectional, minor officials and service employees	Foreman, meter-reader, shop assistant, door-to-door salesman	
(b) Self-employed men (no employees or expensive capital equipment)	Window cleaner, jobbing gardner	'Intermediate'
5 Skilled manual workers (with apprenticeship or equivalent)	—	
6 Other relatively skilled manual workers	Unapprenticed mechanics and fitters, skilled miners, painters and decorators, p.s.v. drivers	'Manual'
7 Semi-skilled manual workers	Machine operator, assembler, storeman	
8 Unskilled manual workers	Farm labourer, builder's labourer, dustman	

TABLE D 2. *Voting intention by age and by white-collar affiliations*

Age	White-collar affiliations (family and job)	Voting intention						
		Lab.	Cons.	Lib.	Uncertain (incline to Lib. or abstain)	Abstain	Total	N[a]
		Percentage						
21–30	Both	64	29	7	0	0	100	14
	Either	68	12	8	4	8	100	25
	Neither	82	9	9	0	0	100	11
31–40	Both	71	14	10	0	5	100	21
	Either	74	11	11	0	4	100	46
	Neither	90	7	3	0	0	100	30
41 +	Both	63	26	5	5	0	99	19
	Either	85	10	0	0	5	100	20
	Neither	85	10	5	0	0	100	20

[a] N = 206. No information on date of birth in the case of one respondent. See also note [c], table 3, and note [a], table 24.

References

Abrams, Mark and Rose, Richard, *Must Labour Lose?* (London, 1960).

Abrams, Philip and Little, Alan, 'The Young Voter and British Politics', *British Journal of Sociology*, vol. 16, no. 2 (June 1965).

Alford, Robert A., *Party and Society* (Chicago, 1963).

Anderson, Perry, 'Problems of Socialist Strategy', in Perry Anderson and Robin Blackburn (eds.), *Towards Socialism* (London, 1965).

Bernstein, B. B., 'A Socio-linguistic Approach to Socialisation: with reference to educability', in D. Hymes and J. Gumperz (eds.), *The Ethnology of Communication* (New York, 1968).

Blau, Peter M., 'Social Mobility and Interpersonal Relations', *American Sociological Review*, vol. 19 (1954).

Blondel, J., *Parties and Leaders* (London, 1963).

Butler, D. E. and Rose, Richard, *The British General Election of 1959* (London, 1960).

Campbell, Angus, Converse, Philip E., Miller, Warren E. and Stokes, Donald E., *The American Voter* (New York, 1960).

Cannon, I. C., 'Ideology and Occupational Community', *Sociology*, vol. 1, no. 2 (May 1967).

Department of Scientific and Industrial Research, *Automation* (London 1956).

Douglas, J. W. B., *The Home and the School* (London, 1965).

Duverger, Maurice, *Political Parties* (London, 1962).

Friedmann, Georges, *Le Travail en Miettes*, 2nd ed. (Paris, 1964).

Goldthorpe, John H. and Lockwood, David, 'Not So Bourgeois After All', *New Society*, vol. 1, no. 3 (1962).

'Affluence and the British Class Structure', *Sociological Review*, vol. 11, no. 2 (July 1963).

Goldthorpe, John H., Lockwood, David, Bechhofer, Frank and Platt, Jennifer, 'The Affluent Worker and the Thesis of *Embourgeoisement*: some preliminary research findings', *Sociology*, vol. 1, no. 1 (January 1967).

The Affluent Worker: Industrial Attitudes and Behaviour (Cambridge, 1968).

Goodman, L. Landon, *Man and Automation* (London, 1957).

Hall, J. and Caradog Jones, D., 'The Social Grading of Occupations', *British Journal of Sociology*, vol. 1 (January 1950).

Hamilton, Richard F., 'The Behaviour and Values of Skilled Workers', in Arthur B. Shostak and William Gomberg (eds.) *Blue Collar World*, (New York, 1964).

Harrison, Martin, *Trade Unions and the Labour Party since 1945* (London, 1960).

References

Hoggart, Richard, *The Uses of Literacy* (London, 1959).

Hyman, H. H., *Political Socialisation* (Glencoe, 1959).

Lipset, S. M., *Political Man* (London, 1960).

Lipset, S. M. and Bendix, Reinhard, *Social Mobility in Industrial Society* (Berkeley, 1959).

Lipset, S. M. and Gordon, Joan, 'Mobility and Trade Union Membership', in Reinhard Bendix and Seymour M. Lipset (eds.), *Class, Status and Power*, (Glencoe, 1953).

Liverpool, University of, Department of Social Science, *The Dock Worker* (Liverpool, 1954).

Lockwood, David, 'The "New Working Class"', *European Journal of Sociology*, vol. I, no. 2 (1960).

'Sources of Variation in Working Class Images of Society', *Sociological Review*, vol. 14, no. 3 (November 1966).

Lockwood, David and Goldthorpe, J. H., 'The Manual Worker', Affluence, Aspirations and Assimiliation', paper presented to the Annual Conferance of the British Socialogical Association, 1962.

McKenzie, R. T. and Silver, A. 'Conservatism, Industrialism, and the Working Class Tory in England', *Transactions of the Fifth World Congress of Sociology*, vol. III (Louvain, 1964).

Ministry of Labour, *Statistics on Incomes, Prices, Employment and Production*, no. 17 (London, 1966).

Moser, C. A. and Scott, Wolf, *British Towns* (London, 1961).

Rose, Richard, *Politics in England* (London, 1965).

Runciman, W. G. '*Embourgeoisement*, Self-Rated Class and Party Preference', *Sociological Review*, vol. 12, no. 2 (July 1964).

Relative Deprivation and Social Justice, (London, 1966).

Timms, D. W. G., 'Distribution of Social Defectiveness in Two British Cities: A Study in Human Ecology', unpublished Ph.D. thesis University of Cambridge (1963).

Wilensky, Harold and Edwards, Hugh, 'The Skidder: Ideological Adjustments of Downward Mobile Workers', *American Sociological Review*, vol. 24 (April, 1959).

Willmott, Peter and Young, Michael, *Family and Class in a London Suburb* (London, 1960).

Woodward, Joan, *Management and Technology*, H.M.S.O. (London, 1958).

Young, Michael and Willmott, Peter, *Family and Kinship in East London* (London, 1959).

Index

94